Preface

This booklet provides an introduction to number representation, computer arithmetic as well information coding within a computer for text, audio data, image data and video data. The topics included in this chapter are:

1. Binary Number System and Other Number Systems

2. Signed Integers, 2's Complement and Floating Point numbers

3. Internal Storage Encoding of Characters: ASCII, EBCDIC, UNICODE

4. Representing Audio, Images and Video

In addition to the above, the booklet includes a large number of examples, short answer questions, multiple choice questions, exercises and answers to most of them.

Although much effort has been put in ensuring that the booklet has no errors, the readers are encouraged to report any errors or comments to gkgupta@acm.org.

G. K. Gupta
Monash University
Clayton, Victoria 3800
Australia
November 2011

Table of Contents

Chapter 1
Number Representation
and Arithmetic

1.1 Introduction

Information when stored or transferred within a computer has to be stored in and travel through electrical circuits. All types of information in a computer are stored as binary symbols. The easiest way to measure what is travelling through an electrical circuit is to measure if there is current in the wire or not. On the other hand, when information is stored on magnetic storage devices, it is stored as a series of magnetised or non-magnetised spots. In both cases, the elementary storage of information involves only two possible states. We have in effect a binary system, the simplest way of representing information.

If we associate the digit 0 with no current and 1 with current in an electrical circuit, groups of circuits can then be used to represent more than one digit. For example a set of four wires may have the currents equivalent to '1101', that is the third wire has no current, the others do.

The binary system is very easy to implement and monitor, and any machine based on this idea is very reliable. The machines that are constructed based on the idea of a binary system are called digital machines as each elementary bit of information is transferred and stored in a series of discrete states.

We now discuss several number systems.

1.2 Number Systems

A number is a representation of a value and certain arithmetic operations may be applied to such values. We first discuss representation of natural numbers; numbers that include a zero and any number that may be obtained by adding one repeatedly to it.

All numbers are written as a sequence of digits. Each digit in a number has two properties that determine how it contributes to the number's value.

1. The digit value, for example in the decimal system the digit value is from 0 to 9.

2. The place value, a multiplier value associated with the position of the digit within the number. For example, the contributions of digits 1 and 9 are quite different in decimal numbers 19 and 91.

Such number systems are also called *positional number systems* because the value of each digit depends on its position.

If we consider a number 123 then we know its value is given by $1 \times 10^2 + 2 \times 10^1 + 3 \times 10^0$ if a decimal system is being used. For a base 4 system, the same number 123 has a value in decimal system of $1 \times 4^2 + 2 \times 4^1 + 3 \times 4^0$ or 27. Therefore, we can see that in the decimal system with 10 digit symbols, the place value of each digit grows from right to left in powers of 10, that is, the rightmost digit starts with the power at 0 and then increment by 1 for every place we move to the left. Similarly, in the base 4 system, the number of digits are four (0, 1, 2 and 3) and the place value of each digit grows from right to left in powers of 4, the base of the number system. Other base values represent numbers in exactly the same way.

We can see that a higher base number system is more compact with fewer digits needed to represent a number while a number system with a lower base usually requires more digits to represent the same number. Computer systems use a binary number system since manipulating binary numbers requires relatively simple electronic circuits although the numbers of digits that the binary systems need to deal with is higher.

When we deal with numbers using a pencil and paper we never think about the maximum size of the number that we can represent but in representing numbers in a computer a fixed amount of storage is allocated to each number. Therefore there is always a largest number that can be represented given the storage. For example, given a number that is represented by 32 bits, the number cannot be any larger than $2^{32} - 1$ (that is, no larger than 4,294,967,295). Thus if a number was allocated 64 bits, we could represent larger numbers and if the allocation was only 16 bits then the largest number that could be represented would be smaller.

A background of the binary numbering system is now presented.

1.2.1 Binary Number System

The primary rule to remember when counting in binary is that there are only two digits, 0 and 1. When counting in decimal we count from 0 to 9 by assigning the digits 0 to 9 to the first place on the right in the number (also called the *units* column). When 9 is reached, no more digits are available in the first place, and therefore to count 10, a 1 is placed in the second place from the right (the *tens* column) and the digit in the units column is reset to 0.

Counting in binary is analogous to counting with ten digits, just simpler. Initially 0 occupies the units column. If we count one, 1 now resides in the units column. So far nothing has changed from counting in decimal. When we count one more, as we have run out of digits for the units column already (we have only two digits), the units column is reset to 0 and a 1 is placed in the next column (the *twos* column) and so on.

The binary equivalents for the first sixteen decimal numbers are given in Table 1.1. From the general properties of number systems we know that it will take four binary digits to represent sixteen numbers since $2^4 = 16$. In the decimal system, four digits can represent $10^4 = 10000$ different numbers from 0 to 9999. We also include equivalent numbers in base 3 and base 7. Three digits are required in base 3 and only two in base 7.

> *Quick question 1*: How many numbers can be represented by three digits in base 3 and two digits in base seven?

The base of a number therefore determines the number of digits used to represent a number. To represent decimal 15, it was necessary to use two decimal digits, in base 7 again only two digits, in base 3 it was required to use three base-3 digits while a binary system required four binary digits (or bits). Two decimal digits can represent up to decimal numbers 99, base 7 two digits can be up to decimal 48, two base-3 digits are up to decimal 8 while two bits can represent a maximum of decimal 3. Base-8 (using digits 0, 1 ..7) and base-16 (using 0, 1, ., 9, A, B, C, D, E, F) are explained in more detail later. These systems are called octal and hexadecimal and have special importance because they are related to the binary system.

Decimal	Binary	Base 3	Base 7
0	0000	000	00
1	0001	001	01
2	0010	002	02
3	0011	010	03
4	0100	011	04
5	0101	012	05
6	0110	020	06
7	0111	021	10
8	1000	022	11
9	1001	100	12
10	1010	101	13
11	1011	102	14
12	1100	110	15
13	1101	111	16
14	1110	112	20
15	1111	120	21

Table 1.1 The first sixteen decimal, binary, base 3 and base 7 numbers

It is worth noting that a number like 16 is not a legal representation of a number in any base lower than 7 since the digit 6, for example, does not exist in base 5.

Quick question 2: What symbols could be used for a base 24 number?

Quick question 3: Is it possible for 955 to be a legal number representation in base 3, octal, base 9 or hexadecimal number?

1.2.2 Terminology

The place value of the rightmost digit in a number is the smallest. It is therefore called the *least significant digit*. The place value of the leftmost digit in a number is the largest. It is therefore called the *most significant digit*.

A binary digit is called a *bit* and a series of eight bits strung together makes a *byte*. With eight bits a byte can represent $2^8 = 256$ different numbers from 0 to 255. A byte may also be used for representing a single alphabetical letter as well as other symbols as discussed in Chapters 3 and 4. Table 1.2 presents further terminology.

Name	Symbol	Number of bytes	How much information?
Byte	B	1	One character
Kilobyte	KB	1024 or 2^{10}	Half a page of text
Megabyte	MB	1024 × 1024 or 2^{20}	A 500-page book
Gigabyte	GB	1024 MB or 2^{30}	About 1000 books
Terabyte	TB	1024 GB or 2^{40}	A library of about a million books

Table 1.2 Size terminology

1.2.3 Processing Binary Numbers

To understand how information is stored and manipulated within a computer, we need to understand how:

- binary numbers are added and multiplied, the two basic arithmetic manipulations a computer must perform,

- the three basic logical manipulations (AND, OR and XOR) are performed which are not discussed in this book and left as an exercise, and

- text based applications, for example word processing, can be carried out with a computer based on binary numbers.

We will start by describing how we can add and multiply binary numbers.

1.2.4 Binary Arithmetic Operations

Addition

We first describe how to add two binary numbers. If more than two numbers need to be added, the problem can simply be broken into adding a series of two numbers.

To add two binary numbers we need to remember the set of four very simple rules of binary addition presented in Table 1.3. The first three are familiar; the fourth is an extension of the third when a 1 is carried.

Addition Rules	Comment
$0 + 0 = 0$	Simple rule
$0 + 1 = 1$	Simple rule
$1 + 0 = 1$	Simple rule
$1 + 1 = 10$	This requires a carry to the next higher digit place

Table 1.3 Simple rules of binary addition

For higher base numbers, like the decimal system, similar rules for addition (as well as multiplication) are often written as a symmetric matrix that is of size 10×10 for the decimal number system. The familiar rules for decimal addition are given in a matrix form in Table 1.4. The first column and the first row are the digits of the decimal system and are the labels for the rows and columns of the matrix. Every cell (row, column) gives the value of the addition which is equal to row digit + column digit.

	0	1	2	3	4	5	6	7	8	9
0	0	1	2	3	4	5	6	7	8	9
1	1	2	3	4	5	6	7	8	9	10
2	2	3	4	5	6	7	8	9	10	11
3	3	4	5	6	7	8	9	10	11	12
4	4	5	6	7	8	9	10	11	12	13
5	5	6	7	8	9	10	11	12	13	14
6	6	7	8	9	10	11	12	13	14	15
7	7	8	9	10	11	12	13	14	15	16
8	8	9	10	11	12	13	14	15	16	17
9	9	10	11	12	13	14	15	16	17	18

Table 1.4 Addition table for the decimal number system

Similarly, the rules of binary addition given in Table 1.5 may now be written as a 2 x 2 matrix in Table 1.5. Once again, the first row and column are only the labels for the rows and columns.

	0	1
0	0	1
1	1	10

Table 1.5 Addition table for the binary number system

The rules are very simple, of course, but it is important to formalise the rules in a table since the representation is useful in dealing with numbers with a higher base, for example, base 16. To add any two numbers, we use the familiar addition technique by starting by adding the two least significant digits and then continue left. We will do so for binary additions.

Example 1.1 Addition of two binary numbers

Consider the problem of adding two binary numbers, one having four binary digits and the other having five.

$$1110$$
$$+ 11100$$

The steps for addition from the right hand side are:

$$0 + 0 = 0$$
$$1 + 0 = 1$$
$$1 + 1 = 0 \text{ (carry 1)}$$
$$1 + 1 + 1 = 1 \text{ we had a carry from the last step (again carry 1)}$$
$$1 + 0 + 1 = 10 \text{ using the carry from the last step}$$

Therefore, the result is 101010. In the last step of the addition above, we assumed that the first number 1110, which is only four binary digits long while the other number is five digits long, may be written as 01110.

We now consider multiplication of two binary numbers.

Multiplication

Just as in decimal multiplication, binary multiplication can be reduced to a set of additions. We first multiply the first number by each digit of the second starting from the right, therefore obtaining a sequence of numbers. We add these numbers to obtain the final value of the multiplication. Although this is simple to conceptualise it is a slow process, as you need to add a series of binary numbers.

We first look at binary multiplication rules. The usual rules are given in matrix form in Tables 1.6. Once again, the multiplication table for binary numbers is rather simple. The only time we get a non-zero result is when 1 is multiplied by 1.

	0	1
0	0	0
1	0	1

Table 1.6 Multiplication table for the binary number system

We now present an example of binary multiplication.

Example 1.2 Multiplication of two binary numbers

Consider multiplying two binary numbers 1101 and 1001. We give the multiplication steps in Table 1.7 in which we multiply the first number by one digit of the second number at a time starting from the right and then add up all these results to obtain the result.

1101 x 1001	
1101	1101 is multiplied by the first digit of 1001
00000	1101 multiplied by the second digit of 1001 and shifted left by one digit
000000	Multiply by the third digit and shift left by one more digit
1101000 -------------	Multiply by the fourth digit and shift left by one more digit
1110101	Add all the results of the multiplications above

Table 1.7 An example of multiplying two binary numbers

It should be understood that shifting by one digit is required when multiplying by a digit that is in the second place and by two digits when multiplying by a digit that is in the third place. For example multiplying 1101 by the leftmost 1 of the number 1001 in the above example is equivalent to multiplying 1101 by a binary number 1000 so shifting by three digits is necessary to get the correct result.

1.2.5 Octal and Hexadecimal Number Systems

The binary numbers used to store information in a computer are frequently 16, 32 or even 64 bits long. The human mind is not good at remembering such large strings of 0s and 1s. To overcome this problem Octal and Hexadecimal number systems have been developed that are compact to help a person in reading, writing and remembering numbers. Numbers in these systems are also very easy to convert to equivalent numbers in the binary system and therefore have a special relationship with the binary numbers.

The basis for the octal and hexadecimal number systems is that the bases of these two number systems are themselves a power of 2; the base is 8 for the octal system and 16 for the hexadecimal. The benefit of using a base that is a power of 2 is that each digit used in such systems may be represented by a small group of binary digits. Conversion from such systems to binary is then straightforward, involving just replacing each octal or hexadecimal digit by its binary representation. For example, octal number 127 may be written in binary by replacing each octal digit by a group of three binary digits as (001)(010)(111) or 1010111 if we ignore the leading digits.

As noted earlier, the octal system uses a base 8, which is 2^3. There are thus eight digit values, which may be written as 0, 1, 2, 3, 4, 5, 6 and 7. In the octal system, each octal digit is equivalent to three binary digits. The place value of each octal digit therefore is 1 (the least significant octal digit) followed by 8^1 (8), 8^2 (64), and 8^3 (512) compared to the decimal system place values of 1, 10, 100, 1000. The representation therefore is compact and easy to convert to binary.

The hexadecimal system (sometimes called *hex*) produces representations that are even more compact by using a base 16 or 2^4. It follows that the hexadecimal system has 16 digits; normally the first 10 digits of the decimal system are used followed by digits A (= 10), B(= 11), C(= 12), D(= 13), E(= 14) and F(= 15). The place value of each hex digit therefore is 1 followed by 16^1 (16), 16^2 (256), and 16^3 (4096) compared to the decimal system place values of 1, 10, 100, 1000. The representation therefore is more compact than the decimal system and easy to convert to binary. For example, the hexadecimal number AB7 may be written in binary by replacing each hexadecimal digit by a group of four binary digits as (1010)(1011)(0111) or 101010110111.

Table 1.8 presents decimal numbers from 0 to 31 and their representations using the binary, octal and hexadecimal systems.

Note that the hexadecimal system is very compact. Two digits in the decimal system can represent from 0 to 99 while two hexadecimal digits can represent decimal numbers 0 to 255.

Now we consider how binary numbers may be converted into decimal numbers and how decimal numbers may be converted to binary.

Decimal	Binary	Octal	Hexadecimal	Decimal	Binary	Octal	Hexadecimal
0	0000	0	0	16	10000	20	10
1	0001	1	1	17	10001	21	11
2	0010	2	2	18	10010	22	12
3	0011	3	3	19	10011	23	13
4	0100	4	4	20	10100	24	14
5	0101	5	5	21	10101	25	15
6	0110	6	6	22	10110	26	16
7	0111	7	7	23	10111	27	17
8	1000	10	8	24	11000	30	18
9	1001	11	9	25	11001	31	19
10	1010	12	A	26	11010	32	1A
11	1011	13	B	27	11011	33	1B
12	1100	14	C	28	11100	34	1C
13	1101	15	D	29	11101	35	1D
14	1110	16	E	30	11110	36	1E
15	1111	17	F	31	11111	37	1F

Table 1.8 Representation of the first 16 decimal numbers in binary, octal and hexadecimal number systems

1.3 Conversion between Different Unsigned Number Systems

Let us look at base conversion between unsigned numbers represented using different base systems starting with conversion from binary numbers to decimal numbers. Two methods are commonly used in conversions. The methods are demonstrated in the next section. We deal only with integers here. Factions are discussed in the next chapter.

1.3.1 Binary to Decimal Conversion

As noted above, two simple algorithms exist for converting a binary number to a decimal number. The two algorithms, Algorithms 1.1 and 1.2, are now described.

Algorithm 1.1 From right to left

This algorithm is straightforward as it essentially multiplies each binary digit by its place value and adds the results. We assume the least significant digit as digit number 1 and the next digit as digit number 2 and so on. The algorithm is described below:

1. Let $S = 0$ and $i = 0$
2. Multiply the next digit (digit $i + 1$) with its place value (2^i). Let the result be v_i
3. $S = S + v_i$
4. Stop if no more digits, otherwise set $i = i + 1$ and go to Step 2
5. Result is S

Note that the first step of the algorithm is the initialization step followed by the second step which computes the value of the first digit and adds it to the sum of the number, then the second digit and adds to the sum, then the third digit and so on until all digits have been evaluated and added to the sum.

This algorithm requires that we know the place values of the binary digits. The place values of the first 11 binary digits from the least significant are given in Table 1.9.

Place	Place value
First	$2^0 = 1$
Second	$2^1 = 2$
Third	$2^2 = 4$
Fourth	$2^3 = 8$
Fifth	$2^4 = 16$
Sixth	$2^5 = 32$
Seventh	$2^6 = 64$
Eighth	$2^7 = 128$
Ninth	$2^8 = 256$
Tenth	$2^9 = 512$
Eleventh	$2^{10} = 1024$

Table 1.9 Place values of digits in the binary number system

We note that the numbers that have the least significant digit 1 are the only numbers that are odd since all other digit values are powers of 2 and are therefore even. All numbers with the least significant digit 0 are even.

Example 1.3 Using Algorithm 1.1

Let us consider an example of converting the binary number 110101 into a decimal number. The steps of the example using Algorithm 1.1 are given in Table 1.10. S is initially zero.

v_i	$S = S + v_i$	Comments
$1 \times 2^0 = 1$	$S = 0 + 1 = 1$	First digit multiplied by its place value and added to S
$0 \times 2^1 = 0$	$S = 1 + 0 = 1$	Second digit multiplied by its place value and added to S
$1 \times 2^2 = 4$	$S = 1 + 4 = 5$	Third digit multiplied by its place value and added to S
$0 \times 2^3 = 0$	$S = 5 + 0 = 5$	Fourth digit multiplied by its place value and added to S
$1 \times 2^4 = 16$	$S = 5 + 16 = 21$	Fifth digit multiplied by its place value and added to S
$1 \times 2^5 = 32$	$S = 21 + 32$	Sixth digit multiplied by its place value and added to S
	$S = 53$	Final value of S is the result

Table 1.10 Using Algorithm 1.1 to convert a binary number to a decimal number

Now we describe the second algorithm to convert a binary number to decimal. In this algorithm we travel from the leftmost digit to the rightmost digit in contrast to the last algorithm which involved travelling from the right to the left.

Algorithm 1.2 From the left to the right

1. Let the most significant (leftmost) binary digit be b
2. Multiply b by 2 and add the next binary digit. That is $b = b \times 2$ + next binary digit.
3. Repeat step 2 until the least significant binary digit has been added
4. b is the result

Example 1.4 Using Algorithm 1.2

To convert the binary number 110101 into a decimal number using Algorithm 2 we follow the steps given in Table 1.11.

Steps	Comments
$1 \times 2 + 1 = 3$	First two most significant digits of 110101 have been used
$3 \times 2 + 0 = 6$	The third digit 0 of 110101 is now used
$6 \times 2 + 1 = 13$	The fourth digit is now used
$13 \times 2 + 0 = 26$	The fifth digit is now used
$26 \times 2 + 1 = 53$	The least significant digit has been finally used and result obtained

Table 1.11 Using Algorithm 1.2 to convert a binary number to a decimal number

A careful reader would have noticed that this algorithm carries out the same computations as Algorithm 1.1 but does them from left to right since the value of the leftmost binary digit is 2^{n-1} if n is the number of digits.

1.3.2 Decimal to Binary Conversion

The algorithms for decimal to binary conversion are essentially the reverse of the algorithms 1.1 and 1.2 presented above. We describe these two algorithms; algorithm 1.3 and algorithm 1.4.

Algorithm 1.3 begins by generating the most significant digit and then moving right. For example, we know that a binary number that has five binary digits must be greater than or equal to 16 and less than 32 (2^4 and 2^5 respectively) since the smallest five bit binary number is 10000 (=16) and the largest is 11111 (=31). Therefore if a decimal number is between 16 and 31, we know that its equivalent binary representation has five bits with the first digit equal to 1. We then subtract the largest power of 2 (2^4) from the decimal number leaving 0000 as the smallest number and 1111 as the largest four-bit number. Now we can apply the same algorithm we used before to find if the next bit is zero or one. Of course at the first step of the algorithm the equivalent binary number must start with a 1.

Algorithm 1.3 From the left to the right

1. Subtract from the decimal number the highest power of 2 (let it be i) that leaves the result 0 or larger.

2. Record a 1 as the most significant binary digit

3. Now subtract from the remainder the i-1 power of 2. If the result is 0 or greater then the next binary digit is 1 otherwise 0.

4. Decrement i and continue Step 3 until i is zero

Example 1.5 Using Algorithm 1.3

We consider an example of converting the decimal number 53 to a binary number using Algorithm 1.3. Since the number 53 is smaller than 64 (2^6) and greater than 32 (2^5), we follow the steps given in Table 1.12.

Subtract next power of 2	Remainder	Next binary digit
53 – 32	21	1
21– 16	5	1
5 – 8	Negative	0
5 – 4	1	1
1 – 2	Negative	0
1 – 1	0	1
Result		110101

Table 1.12 Converting a decimal number to a binary number using Algorithm 1.3

We briefly explain Algorithm 1.3 further. As noted above, we know the binary number must start with the binary digit 1 as the most significant digit (it does not really make much sense to have the most significant digit as zero), which has a place value of 2^i for some value of i. Step 1 of the algorithm determines i. Once the value of i is determined, we can subtract 2^i from the number and find representation for the remainder using the same algorithm.

Algorithm 1.4 From the right to the left

Before describing the algorithm we would like to ensure that the reader is familiar with some simple arithmetic terms used in division. A division may be written as:

Dividend/Divisor = Quotient + Remainder/Divisor

For example, $47/5 = 9 + 2/5$ where 47 is the dividend, 5 is the divisor, 9 is the quotient and 2 is the remainder.

Now we can describe this algorithm. Note that Algorithm 1.3 finds the most significant bit first and then the next significant bit and so on. This algorithm finds the least significant bit first and then the next significant bit and so on. We have noted earlier that the least significant bit in a binary representation is 1 only if the equivalent decimal number is odd. This is the concept used in the algorithm that is now described.

1. Start by setting the quotient to be equal to the decimal number to be converted.

2. Divide the quotient by 2, the remainder is the next binary digit.

3. Use the quotient to do Step 2 repeatedly until the quotient reaches zero.

Example 1.6 Using Algorithm 1.4

We again use the example of finding the binary representation for the decimal number 53. The algorithm steps are given in Table 1.13. Every step involves dividing by two and finding the remainder and continuing with the quotient at the next step.

Quotient divided by 2	Remainder	Quotient
53/2	1	26
26/2	0	13
13/2	1	6
6/2	0	3
3/2	1	1
1/2	1	0
Result	110101	

Table 1.13 Example of Algorithm 2 for converting a decimal number to a binary number

As noted earlier, each odd quotient results in the remainder 1 and therefore the next bit is 1 otherwise the next bit is 0. Perhaps this is a somewhat simpler algorithm than Algorithm 1.3. Note that the algorithm started by finding the least significant bit and then the next bit and so on. That is why the middle column gives bits from right to left.

1.3.3 Converting Binary Numbers to Octal and Hexadecimal

Converting binary numbers to octal or hexadecimal is relatively simple since in each of the two cases a group of binary digits (3 in octal and 4 in hexadecimal) is replaced by one octal or hexadecimal digit.

The conversion method may be described as below:

1. Start from the right hand side of the binary number and group all bits into groups of 3 for octal and groups of 4 for hexadecimal. Zeros may need to be added to the left hand side if the number of bits is not an exact multiple of 3 for octal or a multiple of 4 for hexadecimal.

2. Replace each group of bits with its equivalent octal or hexadecimal digit.

Example 1.7 Binary to Octal and Hexadecimal

We first consider an example of converting the binary number 10110010011010 into an octal number.

Grouping the number in 3 bit groups, we obtain 10 110 010 011 010. Since the first group has only two bits, we change 10 to 010 and may write the number and its octal representation as

(010)(110)(010)(011)(010)
(2)   (6)   (2)   (3)   (2)

So the octal representation is 26232 since 010 binary is 2 octal, 110 binary is 6 octal and so on.

Converting into hexadecimal involves grouping the binary string 10110010011010 to 4 bit groups 10 1100 1001 1010. Again 10 is changed to 0010 and the number and its hexadecimal representation may be written as

$$(0010)(1100)(1001)(1010)$$
$$(2) \quad (C) \quad (9) \quad (A)$$

Thus the hexadecimal representation turns out to be 2C9A since 0010 binary is 2 hexadecimal, 1100 binary is C hexadecimal, and so on.

1.3.4 Converting Octal and Hexadecimal Numbers to Binary Numbers

As shown by our simple examples earlier, this conversion is simpler still since the octal or hex number is converted to binary by replacing each digit by its binary equivalent. We now give an example of how to convert 26232 in octal (we may write it as 26232_8 to ensure there is no confusion) or 2C9A in hex ($2C9A_{16}$) may be converted to binary.

Example 1.8 Octal and Hexadecimal to Binary

We consider an example of converting the binary 26232 octal to an equivalent binary number.

Each octal digit is replaced with three binary digits as shown below.

$$(010)(110)(010)(011)(010)$$
$$(2) \quad (6) \quad (2) \quad (3) \quad (2)$$

Since the most significant binary digit is 0 it may be dropped and we get the equivalent binary number 10110010011010.

Now consider converting the hexadecimal number 2C9A to binary. Each hexadecimal digit needs to be replaced by 4 bits as shown below.

$$(0010)(1100)(1001)(1010)$$
$$(2) \quad (C) \quad (9) \quad (A)$$

Since the two most significant binary digits are zero, they may be dropped and we get the equivalent binary number 10110010011010.

1.3.5 Converting Octal and Hexadecimal Numbers to Decimal Numbers

The algorithms we used earlier for converting binary numbers into decimal numbers may also be used for converting octal or hexadecimal numbers into decimal numbers. We illustrate the method using two examples.

Algorithm 1.5 From right to left

This algorithm is straightforward as it essentially multiplies each octal or hexadecimal digit by its place value and adds the results. We assume the least significant digit as digit number 1 and the next digit as digit number 2 and so on. The algorithm is described below:

1. Let $S = 0$ and $i = 0$
2. Multiply the next digit (digit $i + 1$) with its place value (8^i or 16^i). Let the result be v_i
3. $S = S + v_i$
4. Stop if no more digits, otherwise set $i = i + 1$ and go to Step 2
5. Result is S

Note that the first step of the algorithm is the initialization step followed by the second step which computes of value of the first digit and adds it to the sum of the number, then the second digit and adds to the sum, then the third digit and so on until all digits have been evaluated and added to the sum.

Example 1.9 Using Algorithm 1.5 (Octal to decimal)

Let us consider an example of converting the octal number 6232 into a decimal number. The steps of the example using Algorithm 1.5 are given in Table 1.14. S is initially zero.

v_i	$S = S + v_i$	Comments
$2 \times 8^0 = 2$	$S = 0 + 2 = 2$	First digit multiplied by its place value and added to S
$3 \times 8^1 = 24$	$S = 2 + 24 = 26$	Second digit multiplied by its place value and added to S
$2 \times 8^2 = 128$	$S = 26 + 128 = 154$	Third digit multiplied by its place value and added to S
$6 \times 8^3 = 3072$	$S = 154 + 3072$	Fourth digit multiplied by its place value and added to S
	$S = 3226$	Final value of S is the result

Table 1.14 Using Algorithm 1.5 to convert an octal number to a decimal number

Example 1.10 presents an example of how a hexadecimal number may be converted into a decimal number.

Example 1.10 Using Algorithm 1.5 (Hexadecimal to decimal)

Let us consider an example of converting the hexadecimal number C9A into a decimal number. The steps of the example using Algorithm 1.5 are given in Table 1.15.

v_i	$S = S + v_i$	Comments
$A \times 16^0 = 10$	$S = 0 + 10 = 10$	First digit multiplied by its place value and added to S
$9 \times 16^1 = 108$	$S = 10 + 108 = 118$	Second digit multiplied by its place value and added to S
$C \times 16^2 = 3072$	$S = 118 + 3072$	Third digit multiplied by its place value and added to S
	$S = 3090$	Final value of S is the result

Table 1.15 Using Algorithm 1.5 to convert a hexadecimal number to a decimal number

Algorithm that goes from the left to the right is now described.

Algorithm 1.6 From the left to the right

1. Let the most significant (leftmost) octal or hexadecimal digit be b

2. Multiply b by 8 if octal or 16 if hexadecimal and add the next octal or hexadecimal digit.

3. Repeat step 2 until the least significant octal or hexadecimal digit has been added

4. b is the result

We now present two examples, one to illustrate octal representation numbers into decimal representations and the other to covert hexadecimal representation numbers into decimal representations.

Example 1.11 Octal to decimal

Consider a simple example of converting 6232_8 to decimal.

The steps of this algorithm are similar to the steps used in converting binary to decimal except now the base is 8 instead of 2 for the binary system. The steps are given in Table 1.16.

Step	Comments
$6 \times 8 + 2 = 50$	First two digits of 237 have been used
$50 \times 8 + 3 = 403$	The third digit 3 of 6232 is now used
$403 \times 8 + 2 = 3226$	The fourth digit 2 of 6232 is now used and we are done. The result is 3226.

Table 1.16 An example of converting an octal number to decimal

Example 1.12 Hexadecimal to Decimal

We consider a simple example of converting C9A hexadecimal to decimal. The steps of this algorithm are similar to the steps used in converting Octal to decimal except that now the base is 16 instead of 8 for the octal system. The steps are given in Table 1.17.

Step	Comments
$C \times 16 + 9 = 201$	First two digits of C9A have been used. Note that C stands for decimal 12.
$201 \times 16 + A = 3226$	The third digit A of C9A is now used and we are done. The result is 3226 decimal.

Table 1.17 An example of converting a hexadecimal number to decimal

Summary

In this chapter, we have described how numbers may be represented in binary, octal and hexadecimal and how numbers represented in one base may be converted to equivalent numbers in another base. This included converting decimal numbers to binary representation, binary numbers to decimal representation, octal and hexadecimal to binary representations and to decimal representations as well as converting binary representations and decimal representations to octal and hexadecimal representations. Arithmetic using binary representation numbers has also been described. Counting in bases other than base 10 is similar to counting in decimal. While in decimal, each digit's place value is 1, 10, 100, , the place values are 1, 2, 4, 8,… in binary and 1, 8, 64, 512,… in octal and 1, 16, 256 ..etc in hexadecimal..

Chapter 2
Signed Integers, 2's Complement and Floating Point Numbers

2.1 Introduction

The focus in Chapter 1 was on describing how numbers may be represented in binary, octal and hexadecimal and how numbers represented in one base may be converted to equivalent numbers in another base. Arithmetic using binary representation numbers was also described. We found that counting in bases other than base 10 is similar to counting in decimal. While in decimal, each digit's place value is 1, 10, 100, , the place values are 1, 2, 4, 8,... in binary and 1, 8, 64, 512,... in octal and 1, 16, 256 ..etc in hexadecimal..

Signed numbers involve other issues that we will briefly discuss. There are three commonly used approaches to representing signed integers. These are signed magnitude and complementary numbers. We discuss each of them.

2.2 Signed Magnitude Representation

Since a sign – or + cannot be represented within a computer, one convenient way to represent the sign is to use the leftmost or the most significant bit in the storage area (the storage area may be 16, 32 or 64 bits) to indicate the number's sign. Often a 1 in this bit is used to indicate a negative number. The remaining bits represent the magnitude of the number. This representation, not surprisingly, is called the *signed-magnitude representation.*

Since one bit of say a 32-bit number is used for the sign, the magnitude of the number that can be represented is reduced to $2^{31} - 1$ and thus numbers in the range –2, 147, 483, 647 to +2, 147, 483, 647 may now be represented.

Example 2.1

We now show how an 8-bit integer could use signed-magnitude number representation. Let us look at two signed magnitude binary numbers: 11000011 and 01000011. The magnitude of the two numbers is identical, seven bits 1000011, which is equivalent to decimal number 67. Therefore, the first number represents –67 while the second represents 67.

Table 2.1 presents signed-magnitude representation of all the 16 4-bit binary numbers. The table also shows complementary numbers that we will consider later.

Although humans are used to signed numbers and in carrying out arithmetic on them, performing arithmetic on signed integers on a computer can be complex because the value of an addition or a subtraction is dependent on the signs of the two numbers. We would prefer not having to check the signs to improve the speed of arithmetic. Multiplication and division are not so dependent on the sign so it will be easier to work out algorithms for them. A further complication arises because zero can be represented as either 00000000 or 10000000 in an 8-bit representation. How would a program running on a computer compare the two numbers?

Computers do not use the signed-magnitude numbers to represent signed integers because of the complexity of arithmetic. We now present a number representation system that is the basis of representing signed integers in the computer. It is called the complementary number representation.

Adding Two Signed Magnitude Binary Numbers

The procedure for adding two signed magnitude binary numbers is slightly more complex than adding to unsigned binary numbers since we must now take into account the sign of each number. The procedure for addition is described by the following two steps:

Step 1 – If the signs of the two numbers are the same the both numbers are added and the result's sign is the same as for the two numbers.

Step 2 - If the signs of the two numbers are different then it is necessary to determine which of the number has the larger magnitude. The smaller number is subtracted from the larger one and the result has the same sign as the larger number.

Multiplying Two Signed Magnitude Binary Numbers

The algorithm for multiplying is straightforward and is left as an exercise.

2.3 Complementary Number Representations

The aim of complementary number representations is to carry out computer arithmetic without looking at each number's sign.

Let us first consider four-bit binary numbers given in the first column of Table 2.1. The 16 numbers can represent unsigned decimal integers from 0 to 15 as shown in Column 2. The same binary numbers could be used to represent signed-magnitude numbers from 0 to 7 and 0 to –7 by using three bits for the magnitude and one for the sign. The third column shows this decimal representation of the numbers in the first column.

Numbers in binary	Unsigned numbers in decimal	Signed-magnitude numbers in decimal	1's complement representation of numbers	2's complement representation of numbers
0000	0	0	0	0
0001	1	1	1	1
0010	2	2	2	2
0011	3	3	3	3
0100	4	4	4	4
0101	5	5	5	5
0110	6	6	6	6
0111	7	7	7	7
1000	8	–0	–7	–8
1001	9	–1	–6	–7
1010	10	–2	–5	–6
1011	11	–3	–4	–5
1100	12	–4	–3	–4
1101	13	–5	–2	–3
1110	14	–6	–1	–2
1111	15	–7	–0	–1

Table 2.1 Signed-Magnitude and complementary number systems

For the moment, let us ignore the last two columns of the table. The signed-magnitude number representation in the third column uses half the numbers (eight of them) to represent positive numbers and the other half to represent negative numbers with two different representations for zero. As noted earlier, in this number system, an arbitrary convention that a number with the first binary bit 1 is negative is used but there is no concept of negative numbers in a computer; they are just a set of bits, which could represent any kind of numbers or characters depending on how the computer hardware and software interpret them.

As noted earlier, the major difficulty with the signed-magnitude representation is the complexity of arithmetic since it involves checking the sign of each number. The question therefore arises, is there a different way to represent negative numbers in a computer that will simplify arithmetic? There is indeed a number representation based on the idea of number complements that overcomes this difficulty.

Before defining number complements, we consider a very simple example. Suppose we want to find the value of 8 – 3 which we can say is addition of 8 and –3. If we do not wish to look at the sign of each number, we first find the difference of 9 (which is base 10 – 1) and 3 (= 6) and add it to 8 (= 14) and then add the most significant digit (which is 1) to 4 obtaining 5 which is the correct result. Another possible technique is to find the difference of 10 (for base 10) and 3 (= 7) and add it to 8 (= 15) and reject the carry, leaving us 5 which is again correct. The number 6 is called the *9's complement* of –3 and 7 is called the *10's complement* of –3. The two techniques have been known for a long time and are called *9's complement* and *10's complement* for decimal (base 10) arithmetic respectively. The techniques also work for any number of digits. For example, we use 999 for three digit numbers and 9999 for four digit numbers for 9's complement and 1000 and 10000 for three and four digit numbers for 10's complement.

For example, if we wanted to find the result of 7650 – 323 then we use four-digit arithmetic and first find the difference of 9999 and 323 (= 9676) and add it to 7650 (= 17326). Now we reject the carry and add it to the remaining number obtaining 7327 which is the correct result. In 10's complement, we convert –323 to 10's complement (= 9677) and add it to 7650 obtaining 17327. We now reject the carry and obtain 7327.

Similar techniques can be used for binary (base 2) numbers. The corresponding techniques are called *1's complement* and *2's complement* respectively.

We first define the idea of a complement of a binary number. Any binary number has a 1's complement number that has the 1's in the original binary number replaced by 0's and 0's replaced by 1's. If we compare columns 1 and 4 in Table 2.1, we find that the complement of any number in column 4 is a number with the same magnitude with the sign changed. For example, 5 in binary is 0101 and its complement is 1010 which is –5 in that column. This is 1's complement. Two's complement for a binary number can be obtained by flipping the bits of a given binary number and adding 1 to it. Thus 0011's two's complement is 1101 (1100 + 1) and that of 11100110 is 00011010 (00011001 + 1).

We now note that the fourth column is the 1's complement of the numbers in the third column and the fifth column is the 2's complement of the numbers. Now we discuss how these representations are better suited for computer arithmetic than the signed-magnitude representation.

The beauty of this scheme is, as noted earlier, that computer arithmetic with this representation does not need to worry about the sign of the number. To add two numbers, we just add the 2's complement representation of the numbers and discard any carry. For 1's complement, we add the two numbers and add the carry to the remaining number. We can see that adding positive numbers works fine as long as the sum of the two numbers is below 7 (with a four-bit representation). Adding a positive and a negative number works just as well and so does the addition of two negative numbers.

We now consider three examples to illustrate three different cases of using complementary numbers; adding a positive and a negative number, adding two negative numbers and subtracting a negative number from another negative number. We will only use 2's complement. Using 1's complement is similar.

Example 2.2 Complement Numbers - Subtraction

Subtract 9 from 53.

53 in 8-bit binary is 00110101 and 9 is 00001001. Using 2's complement we first find representation for –9 and then add it to 53. 2's complement representation of –9 can be obtained by flipping bits of 00001001 and adding 1 to the representation of 9. That is 11110111. Now we add the two numbers:

$$00110101 +$$
$$11110111$$
$$=100101100$$

We throw away the last carry from 100101100 and obtain 00101100 which is 44.

Example 2.3 Complement Numbers - Addition

Add –53 to –9.

As noted in the last example, 53 in 8-bit binary is 00110101 and 9 is 00001001. Using 2's complement we first find representation for –53 and –9 and then add them. Complement representations of –53 and –9 are obtained as explained above and we obtain 11001011 and 11110111 respectively. Now we add these two numbers:

$$11001011$$
$$11110111$$
$$=111000010$$

We throw away the last carry from 111000010 and obtain 11000010, which is a negative number given that the most significant bit is 1, and it is 2's complementary representation of 62. Note that binary representation of 62 is 00111110.

Example 2.4 Complement Numbers - Subtraction

Subtract –9 from –53.

Once again, 53 in 8-bit binary is 00110101 and 9 is 00001001. Using 2's complement we first find representation for –53 and then add it to 9 since we need to find –53 – (–9). Complementary representation of –53 is 11001011. Now add the two numbers:

$$11001011$$
$$00001001$$
and obtain $\quad$ =11010100

Since the most significant bit is 1, it is a binary number that is 2's complementary representation of 00101100 which is 44.

Regarding division and multiplication of complementary numbers, two numbers can be divided by using successive subtraction (which, using complements, becomes successive addition); and multiplication can be performed by using successive addition. We do not present further details since these are beyond the scope of this book.

In summary, we note:

1. In the two complementary number systems, the positive numbers are represented in exactly the same way as they are in the signed-magnitude number representation.

2. The 1's and 2's complement representations of negative binary numbers are obtained by inverting all the 0's and 1's of a given number and then adding one when 2's complementary is used.

3. All negative numbers have the most significant bit as 1. Small negative numbers like decimal –1 and –2 have large binary representation with several significant binary digits as 1.

4. In the complementary representation, arithmetic becomes easier since addition does not need to involve checking the signs of the numbers.

2.4 Real Numbers

Real numbers include rational and irrational numbers. Rational numbers are numbers that may be represented as fraction e.g. 8/3. Irrational numbers are those that cannot be exactly represented as a fraction e.g. $\Pi = 3.141592653\ldots$ which is often approximately represented by 22/7.

We now briefly describe how fractions in decimal are converted to binary fractions and binary fractions are converted into decimal fractions. To do the conversions, we need to remember that the place values of digits after the decimal point are 10^{-1}, 10^{-2}, 10^{-3}, and so on. The place values of binary digits after the binary point are 2^{-1}, 2^{-2}, 2^{-3}, and so on. We have already studied algorithms to convert the integer decimal values to binary and binary to decimal; we now briefly discuss how to convert the fractional part.

Algorithm 2.1

To convert decimal fractions to binary fractions we multiply the decimal fraction by 2 and take the carry digit as the next binary bit.

Example 2.5 – Decimal to Binary

Convert the decimal fraction 0.875 to binary. Using the algorithm described above, we carry out the following steps:

$$0.875 \times 2 = 1.750 \text{ (carry bit is 1)}$$
$$0.75 \times 2 = 1.50 \text{ (carry bit is 1)}$$
$$0.50 \times 2 = 1.00 \text{ (carry bit is 1)}$$

We are now finished since the remaining fractional part is zero. The three carry binary digits were 1, 1 and 1 and therefore, 0.875 is equivalent to 0.111 in binary.

Example 2.6 – Decimal to Binary

Convert the decimal fraction 0.234 to binary. Again, using the algorithm described above, we carry out the following steps:

$$0.234 \times 2 = 0.468 \text{ (carry bit is 0)}$$
$$0.468 \times 2 = 0.936 \text{ (carry bit is 0)}$$
$$0.936 \times 2 = 1.872 \text{ (carry bit is 1)}$$
$$0.872 \times 2 = 1.744 \text{ (carry bit is 1)}$$
$$0.744 \times 2 = 1.488 \text{ (carry bit is 1)}$$

and so on.

We are not finished since the fractional part has not become zero. The five carry binary digits are 0, 0, 1, 1 and 1 and therefore the binary equivalent of decimal 0.234 is 0.00111... Note that the process did not terminate even after five steps. It actually may never terminate if decimal fraction 0.234 does not have an exact representation in binary. Try out five more steps and see what happens.

Example 2.7 – Binary to Decimal

Convert binary 0.101 to decimal. The following procedure may be used.

$$0.101 = 1 \times 2^{-1} + 0 \times 2^{-2} + 1 \times 2^{-3}$$
$$= 0.5 + 0 + 0.125 = 0.625$$

Therefore, binary 0.101 is equivalent to decimal 0.625.

Example 2.8 – Binary to Decimal

Convert binary 0.00111 to decimal.

To find the decimal equivalent, we add the values of each digit as follows.

$$1 \times 2^{-3} + 1 \times 2^{-4} + 1 \times 2^{-5} = 0.2175.$$

Compare this result with representation of decimal 0.234 into binary in Example 2.6.

2.5 Floating-Point Binary Numbers

It is clear that a computer must be able to represent real numbers in addition to the integers that we have discussed in Sections 2.1 to 2.3 and in the last chapter.

We are familiar with representation of real numbers by using the decimal point in decimal numbers like 2.35 or 1288.6543. We have also discussed a similar concept of "binary point" (or radix point) in Section 2.4 and we now discuss *floating-point numbers*. In computer representation of numbers, we have a fixed number of bits to represent each number. This was also a problem with integers because we could not represent any integers larger than the maximum integer that was possible given the storage allocated. In floating point representation, the fixed number of bits is often 32 bits but in some cases it may be 64 bits or even 128 bits. Given the fixed number of bits, we have to decide where we would put the "binary point". Given that we wish to represent from very small real numbers to very large ones, representation like 1288.6543 or 0.000012886543 is not satisfactory because representing the second number would waste storage for representing zeros after the decimal point. Instead, we use a "floating" binary point that is equivalent to the scientific notation of numbers, for example 4.25×10^7 or 32.24×10^{-5}.

The floating-point representation of real numbers is composed of the sign, the *mantissa* value and the *exponent* value. The mantissas in the two numbers above are 4.25 and 32.24 respectively and the exponents are 7 and –5 respectively. The numbers are usually normalised by adjusting the exponent to ensure that the mantissa value is between 1 and the number base being used (2 in computer representation). Using decimal numbers, 4.25 as the mantissa value is normalised to 4.25 and 32.24 is normalised to 3.224. The normalised numbers are then represented as 4.25×10^7 and 3.224×10^{-4}. The normalisation allows best use of a given number of mantissa digits, allowing very large and very small numbers to be represented to about the same percentage precision. In computer representation, the mantissa occupies the major part of the fixed length floating point number with the exponent occupying the remaining bits. It should be clear that if the mantissa is occupying the major part of the number then large values of exponent may not be able to be stored since the exponent only has a small number of bits.

The representation is called floating point since the number of digits represented is fixed but the "binary point" floats depending on the value of the exponent.

Our discussion here is based on the IEEE Standard 754 for floating point numbers. This standard is used by most computer systems uses 32 bits for single precision numbers and 64 bits for double precision numbers. The fixed number of bits is used as given in Table 2.2.

	Sign	Exponent	Mantissa	Exponent bias
Single precision	1 (bit 31)	8 (bits 23-30)	23 (bits 0 to 22)	127
Double precision	1 (bit 63)	11 (bits 52-62)	52 (bits 0-51)	1023

Table 2.2 Number of bits used for components of IEEE floating point standard

Most computer systems also allow single precision as well as double precision for higher precision numbers that require more digits in the mantissa.

29

The above table shows the following components of a floating point representation.

1. The sign bit – the value 1 denotes a negative number and 0 a positive number.

2. The exponent and the exponent bias – the exponent field represents both positive and negative exponents using a bias that is added to the actual exponent value. So an exponent of +5 is represented as 127 + 5 in IEEE single precision and 1023 + 5 in double precision. Exponent of zero is stored as 127 and 1023 respectively. The smallest and largest exponents in single precision are –126 and +127 respectively since –127 and +128 exponent values are used for special numbers.

3. The mantissa – the fraction part determines the precision of the number. In IEEE single precision, 23 bits are available although the first bit is never stored since in the binary system the first bit of mantissa is always 1.

Example 2.9 – Floating Point Representation

Let us use the decimal number system to illustrate how the floating-point numbers are represented. Consider two real numbers 1288.6543 and 0.000012886543. Let us assume we have eight decimal digits to represent them. We allocate six of them to the mantissa and two to the exponent. Let us further assume that one digit of the mantissa is used to represent the sign of the number, leaving us five digits for the mantissa.

Normalised mantissa for both 1288.6543 and 0.000012886543 is 0.12886 or 0.12887 (if the last digit is rounded). The two-digit exponent can be 0 to 99. We will add 50 to the actual exponent value allowing us to use exponent values 0 to 49 to represent negative exponents – 50 to –1 and use exponent values 50 to 99 to represent positive exponents 0 to 49. Thus an exponent value of 25 in the floating point representation will represent an actual exponent of – 25 and exponent of 75 will represent 25.

The floating-point representation of the two numbers is +0.12887E54 and +0.12887E46. We have used symbols + and E only to make it easier to understand the notation. Given the eight-digit storage the numbers would look more like 01288754 and 01288746 where the first digit zero is the positive sign and the last two digits are the exponent.

Floating Point Addition

Step 1 – if the exponents of the two numbers are the same then the mantissas of the two numbers are added taking into account the sign of the numbers and the resulting mantissa is then renormalized.

Step 2 – if the exponents of the two numbers are different then the mantissa of the smaller number is modified so that the two exponents become the same. Now add the mantissas taking into account the signs of the numbers and the resulting mantissa is renormalized.

Floating Point Laws of arithmetic

Arithmetic has a number of laws that include Commutativity, Associativity, distributivity and identity. Not all laws hold for floating point numbers because of the representation being approximate.

Floating Point Errors

The floating point representation is only an approximation of real numbers since only a limited number of bits are available for representation. Therefore the representation often involves errors which can be serious in some type of numerical calculations. To reduce errors it is possible to use double precision floating point representation.

2.6 Negative Based Number Systems

We have now considered number systems with base 2, 8, 10 and 16. Are there number systems in other bases that are worth studying? Number systems in all other bases, whether base 6, 23, or 12, all work in exactly the same way except number systems in negative bases. Yes, number systems in negative bases are not only possible but they have some interesting properties. We will discuss them only briefly here because they are interesting. We will only consider base –2. The place values of the digits starting from the least significant digit in base –2 are $(-2)^0$, $(-2)^1$, $(-2)^2$, $(-2)^3$ and so on. These place values therefore are 1, –2, 4, –8 and so on respectively. This implies that both negative and positive numbers could be represented using the same notation without any need for a sign digit. We consider numbers in Table 2.3.

Numbers in base -2	Equivalent numbers in base 10
0001	1
0010	–2
0011	–1
0100	4
0101	5
0110	2
0111	3
1000	–8
1001	–7
1010	–10

Table 2.3 Numbers in base –2 and their base 10 equivalent

Perhaps you would like to try more of these numbers and their decimal equivalents. You could even look at numbers in base –10. How do we tell which of the numbers are negative and which are positive? There is a simple rule: a number with an odd number of digits, after the leading zeros are removed, is always positive and one with an even number of digits always negative since the place value of the most significant digit for such numbers is negative.

Summary

In this chapter we have considered the sign of numbers. Signed numbers involve other issues that we have briefly discussed. There are three commonly used approaches for representing signed integers are signed magnitude and two types of complementary numbers. We discussed each of them. Representation of real numbers in a computer using binary representations has also been discussed.

Chapter 3
Internal Storage Encoding of Characters: ASCII, EBCDIC, UNICODE

3.1 Introduction

Although the binary numbering system is the simplest there is, how can it be used to represent textual information? The answer is the characters are coded in binary bit patterns. We discuss the coding schemes now.

As computers have evolved and the range of applications and languages used have grown, the character codes have also evolved because use of languages like Japanese and Chinese require much richer character codes. The first computer codes used six bits to code characters which could code only 64 characters. The codes were called Binary Coded Decimal (BCD). It was soon discovered that the BCD codes were not sufficient to represent the variety of characters that were required to be used in computer applications.

As noted earlier, the most common grouping of bits is called a byte. It comprises eight bits and therefore can have 256 different values. The reason that a byte is the most common sized grouping is that a byte is typically used to hold and code representations used in textual applications.

To represent information in English (Roman) script we at least need codes to represent 26 upper case (or capital) letters, 26 lower case letters, 10 digits, a few punctuation marks such as comma, period (full stop), minus and plus signs, space, and carriage return. In addition, there are special characters like ~ ! @ # % and a variety of characters that cannot be displayed but are required in the computer. These characters can be mapped to binary numbers using a coding scheme in which a number can represent a character. As noted above, a six-bit code BCD allows only 64 character codes, which is quite inadequate given the number of characters we need codes for; seven bits would allow 128 characters, which might be enough, while eight bits, as noted earlier, would allow 256 characters which appear sufficient for the Roman script. The Chinese, Japanese and Korean (CJK) languages have a large number of characters, some people believe more than 50,000 codes are required. A code discussed later has a large number of codes for these languages.

3.2 ASCII and EBCDIC

With respect to storing textual information in a computer there are two major codes. EBCDIC (Extended Binary Coded Decimal Interchange Code) developed by IBM and ASCII (American Standard Code for Information Interchange) set as a standard by the US government. ASCII is a 7-bit code using the 8th bit for parity checking (although the need for parity bit has now faded and additional characters have been included) while EBCDIC is an 8-bit code that was designed to be used on large IBM mainframes.

An example of a coding of characters by a number of bits is the Morse code. Morse developed a code comprised of dots, dashes and blank signals for communication over telegraph lines. One could consider this as a base 3 system as there are three states. Each letter in the alphabet was assigned a sequence of dots and dashes as a representation. Blank signals were the representation for the end-of-word and end-of-line.

As noted earlier, the EBCDIC code was developed by IBM for mainframes (System/360) in the mid-1960s after the company discovered that the 6-bit Binary Coded Decimal (BCD) code it was using before was very limiting. IBM decided that it was best to extend the 6-bit code to an 8-bit code. IBM continues to use EBCDIC although the code is obsolete now. The code can be represented in a 16 × 16 matrix with the rows representing the first four bits of the number and the columns the second four bits. We show a part of that matrix in Table 18. The part shown below is the bottom left-hand corner of the matrix. To find the code we use the (row, column) of the matrix. For example, the code for A is 1100 0001 and for 9 it is 1111 1001. Note that some cells of the matrix are vacant which means that there is no code there. For example, there are no codes for 10110000 to 10111001. Also, there are no codes for some values in the 0000 column, for example 1000 0000 does not represent any symbol.

Table 3.1 shows coding of some letters and other symbols in EBCDIC.

	0000	0001	0010	0011	0100	0101	0110	0111	1000	1001
1000		a	b	c	d	e	f	g	h	i
1001		j	k	l	m	n	o	p	q	r
1010		~	s	t	u	v	w	x	y	z
1011										
1100	{	A	B	C	D	E	F	G	H	I
1101	}	J	K	L	M	N	O	P	Q	R
1110	\		S	T	U	V	W	X	Y	Z
1111	0	1	2	3	4	5	6	7	8	9

Table 3.1 Part of the EBCDIC code matrix.

Although IBM had decided on using EBCDIC, the code was not universally accepted by the other equipment manufacturers. As a result the ISO devised a code called the American Standard Code for Information Interchange (ASCII). ASCII has 32 control characters, 10 digits, 52 letters (upper- and lower-case), 32 special characters like ! @ # $ % and the space character. Given that ASCII is a 7-bit code and information in a computer is normally grouped in 8-bit bytes, the reader might be wondering how the 7-bit code fits into an 8-bit byte machine. ISO decided to use the eighth bit for error detection. The approach used is called *parity checking*. Parity checking is a simple and basic error checking technique by which the parity bit (the eighth bit) is either turned on or off depending on whether the sum of the other seven bits is even or odd. Parity checking can be even parity checking or odd parity checking. Assume we are using an even parity checking, then a 7-bit number 101 1100 would be represented as 0101 1100 because it makes the sum of the 1's even. A number 100 1100 would be represented as 1100 1100 for the same reason. Therefore parity checking can detect single bit errors in particular in information transmission.

In recent times however computer hardware has become very reliable and parity checking has become less important. The eighth bit is now often used for an extended coding scheme.

We now present a table of some codes using the ASCII system. Only a small number of characters are presented in Table 3.2. The table shows the parity bit as well using even parity.

ASCII	Hexadecimal	Binary
+	2B	0010 1011
8	38	1011 1000
]	5D	1101 1101
a	61	1110 0001
b	62	1110 0010
c	63	0110 0011
$	24	0010 0100
A	41	0100 0001
B	42	0100 0010

Table 3.2 Some alphanumeric symbols and their ASCII codes in hexadecimal and binary

It should be noted again that the computer has no way of knowing that 10101011 represents the symbol +.

3.3 ISCII

Indian languages are very different than English. We have so many different scripts. Most Indian languages do not have upper- and lower-case letters. The codes therefore need to be different. The code developed in India to represent a number of Indian languages is called ISCII (Indian Standard Code for Information Interchange).

Initially a number of organisations in different parts of India were developing their own coding systems for their regional language but in 1991, the Bureau of Indian Standards adopted the ISCII standard. Many companies are now using ISCII for developing products and solutions. This has been made mandatory for data being collected by organizations like The Election Commission, and for projects such as the Land Records Project.

Some ISCII codes are presented in Table 3.3.

	A0	B0	C0	D0	E0	F0
0		ओ	ड़	ऱ	ଭ	EXT
1	ॱ	औ	ण	ल	ॱ	॰
2	ॱ	आँ	त	ऴ	ॱ	१
3	:	क	थ	ऱ़	ॱ	२
4	अ	ख	द्	व	ଭ ा	३
5	आ	ग	ध	श	ि	४
6	इ	घ	न	प	ी	५
7	ई	ङ	ऩ	स	ी	६
8	उ	च	प	ह	ॱ	७
9	ऊ	छ	फ	INV	.	८
A	ऋ	ज	ब	ा	ा	९
B	ऐ	झ	भ	ि		
C	ए	ञ	म	ी		
D	ऐ	ट	य	ॢ		
E	ऍ	ठ	ऱ	ॸ		
F	आँ	ड	र	ॸ	ATR	

Table 3.3 Some ISCII codes
(from http://acharya.iitm.ac.in/multi_sys/exist_codes.php)

3.4 UNICODE

There is yet another code called the Unicode. It has been developed to overcome the difficulty in using EBCDIC or ASCII for non-Roman alphabets used by a majority of the world's population. Unicode standard is an international code, developed and promoted by a non-profit organisation, The Unicode Consortium. It is a coding system designed to support the worldwide interchange, processing, and display of textual information of diverse languages and technical disciplines. Unicode is a 16-bit alphabet which is downward compatible with ASCII. Because Unicode uses 16 bits coding, it can represent 2^{16} (65,536) different codes including the majority of characters used in every language of the world. One might wonder why we need so many different codes. In fact even 64K different codes might not be enough given all the different symbols that have been used through human civilizations. As noted earlier, the Chinese, Japanese and Korean (CJK) pictographic languages pose their own problems since these languages are not character-based. They use a very large number of symbols. These languages themselves may require 50K or more different codes!

37

Table 3.4 Some CJK symbols

Unicode includes codes for many languages including the CJK pictographic languages as well as codes for the following Indian languages: Bengali, Devanagari, Gujrati, Gurmukhi, Kannada, Malayalam, Oriya, Tamil and Telugu. The details of these codes are available online at http://www.unicode.org/charts/. These Indian language codes are based on the 1988 ISCII codes.

Table 3.4 shows some of these codes.

	00	10	20	30	40	50	60	70
0		ऐ	ठ	र	ी	ॐ	ॠ	०
1	ॱ	ऑ	ड	ृ		।	ॡ	Res
2	ॱ	ऒ	ढ	ल	ॕ	–	ॲ	Res
3	ः	ओ	ण	ऴ	ॕ	ॱ	ॳ	Res
4	ऄ	औ	त	ऴ	ॖ	╱	॥	Res
5	अ	क	थ	व	ॖ	Res	॥	Res
6	आ	ख	द	श	ॗ	Res	०	Res
7	इ	ग	ध	प	ॺ	Res	१	Res
8	ई	घ	न	स	ॻ	क़	२	Res
9	उ	ङ	ऩ	ह	ीं	ख़	३	Res
A	ऊ	च	प	Res	ी	ग़	४	Res
B	ऋ	छ	फ	Res	ी	ज़	५	Res
C	ऌ	ज	व	.	ी	ड़	६	Res
D	ऍ	झ	भ	ऽ	ॊ	ढ़	७	ॽ
E	ऎ	ञ	म	ा	Res	फ़	८	Res
F	ए	ट	य	ि	Res	य़	९	Res

Table 3.4 Some Devanagari Unicode Codes
(From http://acharya.iitm.ac.in/multi_sys/exist_codes.php)

38

Altogether Unicode includes some 8K codes for character-based languages and some 40K codes for Chinese, Japanese and Korean languages. The remaining codes are used for mathematical symbols, extensions of pictographic languages and user-defined symbols. Unicode is still not widely used but it is the default character set for the widely used Java programming language.

Summary

In this booklet, we have described how numbers may be represented in binary, octal and hexadecimal and how numbers represented in one base may be converted to numbers in another base. Counting in bases other than base 10 is similar to counting in decimal. While in decimal, each digit's place value is 1, 10, 100, , the place values are 1, 2, 4, 8,... in binary and 1, 8, 64, 512,... in octal. We also discussed a variety of representations for storing unsigned integers, signed integers and real numbers in a computer using binary representations. Finally, we have also briefly introduced language representing textual information including the ASCII, ISCII and Unicode coding schemes as well as representing audio, image and video data in the computer.

Chapter 4
Representing Audio, Images and Video

4.1 Introduction

We have now looked at how to store integers, real numbers and characters in a computer but a computer stores a wide variety of non-numeric and non-text based information including the following:

1. Audio
2. Images and graphics
3. Video

A number of new gadgets like iPhone, iPad, kindle and kindle fire can store a variety of such information. Also, many popular Web sites, for example, *Google Earth*, *Facebook* and *MyTube* also store images, photos and videos. Furthermore, there are a number of software packages and Web sites that allow users to store and share photographs, for example, *Fotolog*, *flickr* or *picassa*. Also, sound, images and video are being increasingly used in many multimedia applications including games. There are even software packages available to compose music or generate animation. It is important to understand how this information is represented in the computer.

We will not describe in detail how these types of information are represented but give a brief introduction.

Since images, music and video normally require much more storage than numbers and text, it is often necessary to compress the information to save on storage and therefore money. In particular, video data can be quite large and in spite of storage being cheap it is necessary to compress it.

Data compression involves algorithms and programs developed to reduce storage required. Some uncompression programs may transform the compressed data to its original form. We therefore briefly discuss compression techniques before discussing computer representation of the audio, image and video information.

4.2 Compression Techniques

Because the data in audio and video information is large, the information is usually not stored as raw data as noted earlier (although music CDs do) since that requires a large amount of storage. For example, at the rate of 50,000 samples per second, $50000 \times 60 \times 60$ (180 million) data elements will need to be stored for one hour of music. Similarly, video involves at least 15 frames a second that are usually stored after compression, given that each frame is information rich. Therefore audio, image and video data is often compressed using data compression techniques. The data compression technique thus is an important component of any method used for representing audio, image and video information. A CD stores 650 MB of information.

We discuss three simple text compression techniques although there are a number of other techniques since text compression is a very important area. We do not discuss the most commonly used compression techniques called LZW and JPEF since they use more elaborate procedures but they have become industry standards. The three techniques we discuss are:

- Keyword encoding
- Run-length encoding
- Huffman encoding

We note that data compression algorithms can be classified either as *lossless* or *lossy*. A lossless technique means that the compressed data may be restored to the original data when required. This is required in many applications, for example, executable code, word processing files, and legal documents. On the other hand for many types of data it is not required to be restored to their original form. These include images, movies, music and other types of signals that may contain a certain amount of noise. Compression techniques that cannot be converted to the original data are called *lossy*. This distinction is important because lossy techniques are usually more effective at compression than lossless methods.

Example 4.1 - Compression

Assume that a 600 Kbyte colour photograph is to be transmitted over a computer network. If the image is compressed using GIF, which is a lossless technique, the compressed file is about half the size, which is about 300 Kbytes. However if the image is compressed using JPEG, which is a lossy technique, the compressed image is only about 50 Kbytes so the file has been reduced by a factor of more than 10 using a lossy technique.

The three techniques listed above are now described.

4.2.1 Keyword Encoding

Keyword encoding is perhaps the simplest compression technique. This technique is based on the idea of replacing each frequently used word with a single character. For example the most common 10 words of the English language are listed in the table 4.1.

Rank	Word	Symbol
1	the	!
2	of	@
3	and	#
4	a	$
5	to	%
6	in	^
7	is	&
8	you	*
9	that	(
10	it	)

Table 4.1. The Ten Most Common English Words and Symbols That Could replace Them

The 10 words above make up almost one-quarter of all the words used in English literature. Therefore replacing each of these words by a single letter (although most of these words are only 2-3 letters long) could achieve substantial savings.

An alert reader would have noted a number of problems with keyword encoding technique. First compression would be effective only if the words being encoded are say more than three letters long. Also, if we are using the letters in the third column for encoding then these letters should not be in the text or some other scheme must be designed to indicate that the letter actually exists in the text and is not a code. There is also the problem of differentiating between letters starting with upper case letter and those with lower case letters, for example, "That" and "that".

4.2.2 Run Length-Encoding

To understand run-length encoding, it should be noted that data frequently contain the same character repeated many times in a row. It may be that there are multiple spaces to separate sentences or format tables or equations. Some signals may have a run of the same value indicating that the signal is not changing. As an example, music in digital form may have a long run of zeros between songs. Run-length encoding uses this concept in compressing data.

The technique works as follows. Each time a run of same values is encountered, it is replaced by two values. The two values indicate that a run length of a character with a given value is beginning. If the average run-length is longer than two, compression will take place.

Example 4.2 Run Length Encoding

We consider a data set 1,2,3,4,2,2,2,2,4, that we wish to compress and the compressed file generated by the run length encoding algorithm is 1,2,3,4,2,-3,4. The compression program simply transfers each number from the input file to the compressed file, with the exception of the run: 2,2,2,2. This is represented in the compressed file by the two numbers: 2,-3. The first number ("2") indicates what character the run consists of. The second number ("-3") indicates the number of characters in the run, found by taking the absolute value and adding one. For instance, 4,-2 means 4,4,4; 21,-4 means 21,21,21,21,21, etc.

4.2.3 Huffman Encoding

Huffman coding is a technique for constructing variable-length codes. The coding takes as input the frequencies that the code words have and constructs a code that minimizes the weighted average of the code word lengths. This is a form of lossless data compression.

It has been found that most files have only a limited number of characters although most codes like EBCDIC allow 8 bits for each character and therefore 256 codes. For example, if a file was using only two characters and both were equally frequent then the most efficient coding scheme needs only one bit since the two characters may be coded using one of them as 1 and the other as 0. Now consider three characters with one of the characters with a frequency of 50% and the other two each with a frequency of 25% each then the best code would 1 for the frequent character and 00 and 01 for the other two. Note that if one character has a code of 1 then the others must start with 0 since a code like 10 or 11 cannot be used since when the computer finds a 1 it assumes that the character is the frequent one and assumes that the next bit is another letter (or start of another letter). Therefore 10 will be decoded as the most frequent character followed by another character that has a code starting with 0 and 11 will be decoded as one frequent character followed by another frequent character.

Example 4.3 Huffman Coding

Consider a file that has 35 frequent characters and a number of other characters that are less frequent. One possibility is to use five bits to represent most of the frequent characters. Five bits can represent 32 different characters and therefore 31 of the 35 frequent characters and the 32nd five-bit code can be used to help represent the remaining characters. Let us consider how this might work.

First we consider how the 31 most frequent of the 35 characters may be represented. We can use codes like 00000, 00001, 00010, 00011 etc to represent the most frequent characters, we assume, a, b, c, d, e etc respectively. If the 31 most frequent characters represent 90% of the file then we have already achieved 5/8 for 62.5% because ASCII coding would have used 8 bits for each character. We now consider codes for the remaining characters.

Let us assume that the 32nd unused five-bit code is 11111. For the remaining characters, the coding therefore must start with 11111 followed perhaps by the ASCII 8-bit code. This means that characters other than the top 31 will require 13-bits. On the average therefore it is necessary to use $0.9 \times 5 + 0.1 \times 13 = 4.5 + 1.3 = 5.8$ bits. Therefore this coding achieves 2.2/8 = 0.275 or compression by 27.5%.

A good example of Huffman Coding is the country codes for various countries. Since USA and Canada had the largest telephone traffic when the codes were designed, they have a single digit country code followed by a three digit area code. Caribbean countries also have country codes starting with 1 followed by a three digit code. All other country codes are two digits but some country codes which have low international telephone traffic have three digits or more.

Huffman encoding therefore involves coding characters that occur most often allocated as few as one or two bits. Infrequently used characters may require a dozen or more bits. Also, these variable length codes can be packed together. Imagine receiving a serial data stream of ones and zeros. If each character is represented by eight bits, you can directly separate one character from the next by breaking off 8 bit chunks. Now consider a Huffman encoded data stream, where each character can have a variable number of bits. How do you separate one character from the next? The answer lies in the proper selection of the Huffman codes that enable the correct separation. An example will illustrate how this works.

When uncompression occurs, all the eight bit groups are placed end-to-end to form a long serial string of ones and zeros. Look closely at the encoding table of Fig. 27-3, and notice how each code consists of two parts: a number of zeros before a one, and an optional binary code after the one. This allows the binary data stream to be separated into codes without the need for delimiters or other marker between the codes. The uncompression program looks at the stream of ones and zeros until a valid code is formed, and then starting over looking for the next character. The way that the codes are formed insures that no ambiguity exists in the separation.

To implement Huffman or arithmetic encoding, the compression and un-compression algorithms must agree on the binary codes used to represent each character (or groups of characters). This can be handled in one of two ways. The simplest is to use a predefined encoding table that is always the same, regardless of the information being compressed. More complex schemes use encoding optimized for the particular data being used. This requires that the encoding table be included in the compressed file for use by the uncompression program. Both methods are common.

4.3 Representing Audio Data

Audio data is transmitted to humans by sound waves. When two people are talking, the speaker's speech essentially generates sound waves that the other person's eardrum picks up when it vibrates which sends signals to the brain. Hi-fi equipment also generates sound waves when its electronic circuitry sends signals to the speakers. The speaker causes a membrane to vibrate which in turn generates waves in the surrounding air. The human ear picks up the waves generated by the speakers. When listening to audio from a computer, the computer coverts digital audio data into analogue signals which are sent to its speakers that in turn generate the sound waves picked up by the human eardrums. To store audio data in a computer, it is necessary to digitize the sound wave since the computer represents everything by binary values and therefore it cannot store a continuous audio signal. The signal must therefore be digitised[1] by sampling (as many as 50,000 samples may be taken every second!) and representing the samples by digital values. To replay, the digital values are converted to a continuous analogue signal that is then relayed to the audio speakers. A compact disc (CD) also stores sampled audio information that it converts to analogue form while it is playing before sending it to the speakers.

We note that a vinyl record is an analogue representation of the music. The sounds are recorded in a spiral which is played by the needle going up and down in the spiral thus tracking the analogue signal. Vinyl records are obsolete now and have been replaced by CDs which store audio information digitally. The surface of the CD represents a large number of bits which may be played by a laser reader that can read the binary digits from the surface. These bits are picked up by a receptor which transforms them and sends them to the speaker.

There are a number of formats to represent audio. Some of the formats include AU, AIFF, VQF and MP3. These formats represent audio data in different ways and they use different compression techniques but the most commonly used format is MP3 that offers a high compression technique.

The most widely used format for audio signals is MP3. MP3 provides strong data compression, reducing audio files to about a tenth of the size it would take to store the raw data, and still maintaining an acceptable level of audio quality. MP3 was developed in Germany by the Moving Picture Experts Group (MPEG) and was released in 1992. MP3 compression is *lossy* in that the original data cannot be recovered after the data has been compressed in contrast to a *lossless* technique, like that used for zip files, in which the original data may be recovered. MP3 has become increasingly popular because of devices like the iPod.

---

[1] Continuous information (called analogue information) is converted into digital information by using a device called an analogue-to-digital (or A-to-D) converter. To do the opposite a D-to-A converter is used.

An MP3 encoded file consists of a series of audio frames (like film clips), there are about 40 frames per second. Each frame is encoded based on what sounds humans can hear and what they cannot. Since humans cannot hear outside the 20Hz to 20000Hz frequency band (in fact, our ears are most sensitive to frequencies between 2000Hz and 4000Hz because this is the normal range of human voice and we can barely notice a difference of around 2Hz), all sounds outside the 2-200 Hz range are discarded since there is no point in storing information that humans cannot hear.

Further details of MP3 are beyond the scope of this book. An interested reader should refer to the references given in the bibliography at the end of this chapter.

4.4 Representing Images and Graphics Data

Photographs and graphics and drawings are very different than audio data. As we discussed earlier, audio data is a sound wave that may be stored in analogue or digital form and is always played in analogue form using one or more speakers. The issues faced in representing images and graphics data are quite different than in representing audio data. One of the issues that must be faced is representation of colour and the other issues include representing visual data digitally.

Storing visual information on the computer involves additional issues including the issue of storing colours. Humans perceive colour based on the various frequencies of light that reach the retinas of our eyes. The receptors in the eyes correspond to red, green and blue colours. All other colours are made by combining the three colours. Computers also use three colours (called RGB) and combine them by providing proportions of each colour by a number between 0 and 255 (8 bits) which then specifies the colour of each pixel in the image. For example, RGB values of (0, 0, 0) specify black, (255, 255, 255) specify white and (255, 130, 255) specify pink. This allows $256 \times 256 \times 256$ (about 16 million) different colours to be specified, many more than the human eye can distinguish.

Representing an image in a computer involves storing each dot (called a *pixel*) of the image. The more pixels the computer stores for an image, the better the resolution. Digital cameras for example offer 3, 4 or even 10 megapixel resolution which means that a 4 megapixel image has equivalent of 2000×2000 pixels. Digital camera images however are not square, for example, a Canon 7.1-megapixel camera has an image size of 3072×2304 and the Canon EOS-1DS 11-megapixel camera image is 4064×2704 pixels. Storing such large number of pixels for each image requires a lot of memory. For example, using a 4-megapixel image would require 4000000×3 bytes (assuming 3 bytes of RGB information for each pixel) which is 12 Mbytes. If a video camera was shooting 30 frames per second, we would need 360 Mbytes per second or more than 20 Gbytes per minute! We can however see opportunities for saving on storage. For example, three bytes per pixel for its colour appears unnecessary; we do not need 16 million possibilities for each pixel's colour when its colour would normally be similar to that of its neighbours. Similarly, a video frame will be closely related to the previous and the next frame. Unfortunately, we are not able to look into any of the compression techniques in this course.

Colours

Colour is perceived by humans based on the various frequencies of light that reach the retinas of their eyes. The retinas have three types of colour photoreceptors that react to different set of frequencies. The three types correspond to frequencies of colours red, green and blue (RGB). Therefore the common way to model colour in representing computer images is the RGB colour model. This corresponds to the way both the CRT monitors and the LCD monitors reproduce colour. Each pixel is represented by three values, the amount of red, green and blue. All other colours can be made by combining various amounts of the three RGB colours. The values are given on a scale of 0 to 255, 0 meaning no contribution while 255 means full contribution. RGB value of (255, 0, 0) is red, (157, 95, 82) is purple and RGB value (255, 255, 0) with no contribution from blue is bright yellow. A very large number of colours may be represented in the RGB scheme; many more than the human eye can distinguish or a monitor can display.

Each number in the RGB scheme is assigned three bits to capture a value from 0 to 255. An RGB colour image therefore uses three times as much memory as a gray-scale image of the same pixel dimensions.

Types of Images

There are many types of images. A photograph is an analogue representation of an image although digital photographs are digital representations in which the image is a collection of individual dots called pixels (for picture elements). Each pixel is composed of only a single colour. A high resolution picture has many more pixels than a low resolution picture. Some older mobile phones have cameras that take pictures that have only one million pixels (better cameras are usually been provided now) while some of the hand held cameras can have as many as 15 million pixels. A very expensive camera (Seitz) has recently been advertised that provides 160 millions. The digital image can be converted into analogue representation when printed.

Image Representation

There are two methods for representing images in computers. The first method is called the raster-graphics format and the other is called vector graphics. Raster graphics is a method that uses pixel-by-pixel storage while vector graphics describes an image by using lines and geometric shapes.

Most popular representations of images use raster graphics. These include BMP (bitmap), GIF (Graphics Interchange Format), JPEG (Joint Photographers Expert Group) and MPEG. These formats store images differently and compress them differently. For example, BMP stores pixel colour values of an image from left to right and from top to bottom and supports 24-bit TrueColor. The file can be compressed. GIF was developed in 1987 and only uses 256 colours although each image may be made up of a different set of 256 colours. GIF files are therefore smaller. JPEG uses all the 16 million colours but averages out the colour hues over short distances. Compression may be used to reduce the size of JPEG files.

As noted above, vector graphics uses a format to describe an image in terms of lines and geometric shapes but vector graphics is not suitable for images like photographs.

4.5 Representing Video Data

In some ways video is the most complex data that needs to be represented in a computer. As noted earlier, a video consists of a number of still images per second which when played quickly one after another give our eye a perception of motion. Although a format like GIF could be used for video, the most popular video formats are Quicktime, MPEG and Real Video. We will not discuss the details of these schemes.

Video therefore must be compressed. The techniques for video compression are called codecs which reduces the size of a video substantially using a block oriented lossy compression technique. These techniques divide each video frame in a rectangular block which is then encoded. Hardware as well as software may be used to compress and uncompress. Some popular video codecs are Cinepak, MPEG and Real Video.

Video data is usually stored on a DVD of 4.7 GB but up to 17 GB may be stored using some formats.

Summary

In this booklet, we have described how numbers may be represented in binary, octal and hexadecimal and how numbers represented in one base may be converted to numbers in another base. Counting in bases other than base 10 is similar to counting in decimal. While in decimal, each digit's place value is 1, 10, 100, , the place values are 1, 2, 4, 8,... in binary and 1, 8, 64, 512,... in octal. We also discussed a variety of representations for storing unsigned integers, signed integers and real numbers in a computer using binary representations. Finally, we have also briefly introduced language representing textual information including the ASCII, ISCII and Unicode coding schemes as well as representing audio, image and video data in the computer.

Bibliography

1. T. C. Bell, *Text Compression*, Prentice Hall 1990.

2. N. Dale and J. Lewis, *Computer Science Illuminated*, Jones and Bartlett Publishers, 2007.

3. I. Englander, *The Architecture of Computer Hardware and Systems Software: An Information Technology Approach*, Third Ed., Wiley 2003.

4. J. R. Gregg, *Ones and Zeros: Understanding Boolean Algebra, Digital Circuits, and the Logic of Sets*, IEEE Press, 1998.

5. D. W. Matula, Finite Precision Number Systems and Arithmetic, Cambridge University Press, 2010.

6. L. Null and J. Lobur, *The Essentials of Computer Organization and Architecture*, Jones and Bartlett, 2003.

7. C. M. White, Binary Number System Tutorial, 2003 facweb.cs.depaul.edu/cwhite/Binary%20Tutorial.rtf

8. The binary system, http://www.math.grin.edu/~rebelsky/Courses/152/97F/Readings/student-binary.html

9. S. Hacker, *MP3: The Definitive Guide*, O'Reilly

10. Anonymous, Chapter 2. Audio Fundamentals http://www.gnuware.com/icecast/chap_02.html

11. D. Salomon, *A Concise Introduction to Data Compression*, Springer, 2008.

12. K. Sayood, *Introduction to Data Compression*, Third Edition, Morgan Kaufmann, 2005.

13. The Open University, Representing and Manipulating Data in Computers, http://openlearn.open.ac.uk/mod/oucontent/view.php?id=397589

Chapter 5
Questions and Answers

5.1 Short Answer Questions

1. What digits are used in the binary number system?

2. Why is binary number used in digital computers?

3. What is a Gigabyte and what is a Terabyte?

4. What is the result of adding 101 and 111?

5. What is the result of multiplying 11 by 10?

6. What is binary number 111 in decimal?

7. What is decimal number 11 is binary?

8. What are the digit values of the two digits 1 and 1 in the number 101 if the number is a binary number, octal number, decimal number or a hexadecimal number?

9. Why do we need a binary number system?

10. Covert the decimal number 10 to binary

11. Convert the binary number 10101 to decimal, octal and hexadecimal

12. What does ASCII stand for?

13. How many bits does the ASCII code need?

14. How many bits does the Unicode require?

15. What is ISCII?

16. What digits are used in an Octal number system?

17. How many bits in a hexadecimal digit?

18. List all number systems in which 341 is not a legal number.

19. What is the result of converting 110101011 into Octal?

20. How many Megabytes in a Terabyte?

21. Give the binary representations for decimal numbers six, nine and fifteen.

22. Complete the following binary additions showing all carries in your working.
    - a. $011001 + 001101$
    - b. $110111 + 101010$

23. Convert 101001_2 to base 10

24. Convert 139_{10} to base 2

25. Convert 149_{10} to base 5

26. Convert to hexadecimal: 1011001011111010_2

27. Covert to octal 101110011_2

28. Covert to hexadecimal 357_8

29. Add the binary numbers 10 and 11 and show the result

30. Multiply the binary numbers 10 and 11 and show the result

31. What is lossless compression?

32. What is lossy compression?

33. What type of compression is usually used in audio and video data?

34. What are three different types of compression techniques discussed in this booklet?

35. What type of data is run-length encoding good for?

36. Which one of the three compression techniques lossless?

37. What is RGB? What is it used for?

38. What is raster graphics?

39. What type of representation is GIF and JPEG?

40. Is a clock that has an hour hand and a minute hand an analogue device?

41. How many bits are required to represent a pixel's colour?

42. Represent the following using run-length encoding: AAAAABCCCDDDDDEFFFF

43. How do humans perceive sound?

44. Explain the difference between the quality of images generated by camera that use 1 million pixels, 5 million pixels and 160 million pixels.

45. What is vector graphics? Can photographs be represented using vector graphics?

5.2 Multiple Choice Questions

Basic Questions

1. Which one of the following number bases is used to represent information in a computer?
   (a) Base 2
   (b) Base 8
   (c) Base 10
   (d) Base 16
   (e) None of the above

2. Which one of the following shows the correct conversion of the binary number 01111 into decimal?
   (a) $0 + 1 + 1 + 1 + 1 = 4$
   (b) $0 + 8 + 4 + 2 + 1 = 15$
   (c) $0 + 1000 + 100 + 10 + 1 = 1111$
   (d) $0 + 16 + 8 + 4 + 2 = 30$
   (e) None of the above

3. Which of the following is the place value of the digit 4 in number 1234321_6?
   (a) 64
   (b) 216
   (c) 256
   (d) 8

(e) None of the above

4. Which one of the following is the place value of digit 3 in 0.123_4?

    (a) 1/64
    (b) 1/125
    (c) 1/216
    (d) 1/256
    (e) None of the above

5. Which one is the decimal representation of the 4-bit binary number 0110?

    (a) 12
    (b) 10
    (c) 8
    (d) 6
    (e) None of the above

6. Which one is the correct representation of the decimal number 250?

    (a) 1111 1010 in binary
    (b) 1000 0011 in binary
    (c) EAA in hexadecimal
    (d) 374 in octal
    (e) None of the above

7. Which one of the following is the correct decimal representation for the 8-bit binary number 1111 1111?

    (a) 255
    (b) 256
    (c) 127
    (d) 511
    (e) None of the above

8. Which one of the following is the correct octal representation for the decimal number 247?

    (a) 387_8
    (b) 377_8
    (c) 367_8
    (d) 357_8
    (e) None of the above

9. Which triplet of digits (one digit from each number) in 10234_4, 56789_{10} and $ABCDE_{16}$ has the same place value?

    (a) 1, 5 and A
    (b) 4, 9 and E
    (c) 2, 7 and C
    (d) 1, C and 6
    (e) None of the above

10. Which one of the following is NOT equivalent to 1152_{10} ?

    (a) 10010000000_2
    (b) 102000_4
    (c) 2200_8

(d) 800_{12}
(e) All are equivalent

11. Which one of the following is the binary representation of 512_{10}?
    (a) 1000000000
    (b) 1010010100
    (c) 100000100
    (d) 10000000
    (e) None of the above

12. How many bits are needed to represent 7654_8? Estimate without converting the number to binary.
    (a) 10
    (b) 12
    (c) 14
    (d) 16
    (e) None of the above

13. How many decimal digits are needed to represent $ABCD_{16}$? Estimate without converting the number to decimal.
    (a) 4
    (b) 5
    (c) 6
    (d) 7
    (e) None of the above

14. Which one of the following is the binary representation of 1234_{16}?
    (a) 0011011100
    (b) 1010011100
    (c) 1001000110100
    (d) 1000100001100100
    (e) None of the above

15. Which one of the following is the binary representation of 1234_8?
    (a) 0001101111
    (b) 1010011100
    (c) 1001000110100
    (d) 1000100001100100
    (e) None of the above

16. Which one of the following is the result of adding binary numbers 1110011 and 110011?
    (a) 10001110
    (b) 10100110
    (c) 10100001
    (d) 11010110
    (e) None of the above

17. Which one of the following is the result of adding binary numbers 10101010 and 110011?

(a) 10001110
(b) 10100110
(c) 10100001
(d) 11011101
(e) None of the above

18. Which one of the following is the result of adding 777_8 and 666_8?
    (a) 1665_8
    (b) 1645_8
    (c) 12345_8
    (d) 2645_8
    (e) None of the above

19. Consider the following binary floating-point number format that uses 16 bits. The mantissa is 10 bits normalised such that it consists only of a fraction part (for example, 0.1010101 with leading bit 1) and is represented in sign-magnitude format (a total of 11 bits although the sign bit is represented separately). Therefore, a ten-bit mantissa 0.1010101001 is represented without a binary point as 1010101001 and a sign bit which is 0 if positive and 1 if negative. The exponent has five bits, 16 is added to the actual exponent value allowing exponent values of -16 to +15 to be represented. Therefore exponent of 5 is represented as exponent value $16 + 5 = 21 = 10101_2$. The final representation is the sign bit + exponent + normalized mantissa.

    Which one of the following is the binary floating-point representation of 1100.101010 using the format described above?
    (a) 1101001100101010
    (b) 0.11001010110100
    (c) 111001010110100
    (d) 11001010110100
    (e) None of the above

20. Which one of the following is the binary floating-point representation of 1100.10101010 using the format described above?
    (a) 0110010101010100
    (b) 0.11001010110100
    (c) 111001010110100
    (d) 011001010110100
    (e) Cannot be exactly represented given the format

21. Which one of the following is the one's complement binary representation of -128_{10} using 16 bits to represent it?
    (a) 1000000010000000
    (b) 1111111101111111
    (c) 1111111111111110
    (d) 0000000010000000
    (e) None of the above

22. Which one of the following is the two's complement binary representation of 128_{10} using 16 bits to represent it?
    (a) 1111111110000000

(b) 1111111101111111
(c) 1111111111111110
(d) 0000000011111111
(e) None of the above

23. Which one of the following codes uses 16 bits to represent a character:
    (a) ASCII
    (b) Unicode
    (c) EBCDIC
    (d) ISCII
    (e) None of the above

24. Which one of the following is a format for audio information?
    (a) JPEG
    (b) Quicktime
    (c) MP3
    (d) GIF
    (e) None of the above

25. Which one of the following is not part of a floating point representation
    (a) Mantissa
    (b) Exponent
    (c) Fixed number of bits
    (d) Normalizing mantissa and exponent
    (e) All of the above

26. A DVD has capacity of 1GB. How long a movie can it store with using any compression?
    (a) 25 minutes
    (b) 50 minutes
    (c) 75 minutes
    (d) over 100 minutes
    (e) None of the above

27. Which one of the following is NOT true about binary integer representation?
    (a) Signed magnitude, one's complement and two's complement represent the positive numbers in the same way
    (b) To add two complement numbers we add them in the usual way and ignore the carry beyond the leftmost bit
    (c) To add two complement numbers of the same sign also we add them in the usual way and ignore the carry beyond the leftmost
    (d) To represent a negative binary number in 1's complement form, all the bits of the number are flipped.
    (e) None of the above

28. Which one of the following is correct?
    (a) A binary number may be converted into hexadecimal by reading each group of four binary digits from left and replacing it with an equivalent number in hexadecimal
    (b) A byte cannot store two hexadecimal numbers
    (c) It is not possible to convert a number in base 13 to binary

- (d) A large integer which is too large to be stored as an integer may be approximately stored as a floating-point number
- (e) None of the above is correct

29. Which one of the following is correct?
    - (a) When using signed-magnitude number representation, there are two representations of zero
    - (b) When using 2's complement, there are two representations of zero
    - (c) 2's complement may be obtained by adding two to 1's complement
    - (d) 2's complement is very similar to the signed-magnitude number representation
    - (e) None of the above is true

30. Which one of the following statements is true?
    - (a) There is one universally accepted standard for representing characters on a computer, that is ASCII
    - (b) There is one universally accepted standard for representing punctuation on a computer, that is EBCDIC
    - (c) There is one universally accepted standard for representing Indian scripts
    - (d) There is one universally accepted code that can represent the Chinese, Korean and Japanese symbols as well as Roman and Indian scripts
    - (e) None of the above

31. Which one of the following is true for the original ASCII codes?
    - (a) It was a 7-bit code
    - (b) It was a 8-bit code
    - (c) It represented 256 characters
    - (d) It represented only 127 characters
    - (e) None of the above

32. Which one of the following is the correct ASCII code of 'A'?
    - (a) Decimal 66
    - (b) 41 in hexadecimal
    - (c) 0100 0010 binary
    - (d) 0110 0011 binary
    - (e) None of the above

33. Which one of the following is the correct ASCII code of zero?
    - (a) 48 decimal
    - (b) 32 hexadecimal
    - (c) 0011 1000 binary
    - (d) 42 in Octal.
    - (e) None of the above

34. Which two of the following are equivalent to decimal number 48?
    - (a) 110000_2
    - (b) 231_4
    - (c) 60_8
    - (d) 40_{16}
    - (e) All of the above are correct

35. Which two of the following are not equivalent to decimal number 31?
    - (a) 61_6
    - (b) 11111_2
    - (c) 31_8
    - (d) $1F_{16}$

(e) All are equivalent

36. Which one of the following is NOT correct?
    (a) A six digit number $ABCDEF_{16}$ can be represented by an eight-digit octal number
    (b) A six digit number 321000_4 can be converted to an equivalent 12-digit binary number
    (c) Any six digit binary number can be converted into an equivalent 2-digit number in base 8
    (d) A four-digit base 32 number can be represented by eight-digit hexadecimal number
    (e) All of the above are correct

37. Which one of the following is the number of different colours that may be represented using the RGB scheme that uses one byte for each of the three colours?
    (a) 8 x 8 x 8 (or 512 different colours)
    (b) 16 x 16 x 16 (4096)
    (c) 32 x 32 x 32 (32768)
    (d) 64 x 64 x 64 (262,144)
    (e) None of the above

38. Which one of the following is NOT correct?
    (a) An audio signal is digitized by sampling an analogue signal at regular intervals
    (b) GIF for images uses 256 colours
    (c) JPEG for images uses all the 16 million colours
    (d) 3 megapixel photo with full colour is 9 Mbytes in size
    (e) All of the above are correct

39. The largest negative number that can be stored in a 16-bit 2's complement form is
    (a) -65536
    (b) -32768
    (c) -16384
    (d) -8192
    (e) None of the above

40. The 2's complement 8-bit representation of number -1 is
    (a) 01111111
    (b) 10000000
    (c) 10000001
    (d) 11111111
    (e) None of the above

Advanced Questions

41. Which one pair or two pairs of digits (one digit from each number) in 1023_4 and 4567_8 have the same place value?
    (a) Only 1 and 5
    (b) 1 and 5 and also 3 and 7
    (c) Only 3 and 7
    (d) Only 1 and 4
    (e) None of the above

42. How many bits do you need to represent one million different numbers?

(a) 7
(b) 10
(c) 15
(d) 20
(e) None of the above

43. How many decimal digits are needed to represent the 16-bit number
1010101010111100_2? Estimate it without converting the number to decimal.
    (a) 3
    (b) 4
    (c) 5
    (d) 6
    (e) None of the above

44. Hows many bits are needed to represent 123456_{10}? Estimate without converting the
number to binary.
    (a) 17 or 18
    (b) 15 or 16
    (c) 13 or 14
    (d) 19
    (e) None of the above

45. Which one of the following is the binary representation of 1234_{32}?
    (a) 1001000110100
    (b) 0001010011100
    (c) 1001000110100
    (d) 1000100001100100
    (e) None of the above

46. When 791 is represented in bases 2, 4, 8, and 16, which two of the following
representations have no zeros in them?
    (a) Base 2
    (b) Base 4
    (c) Base 8
    (d) Base 16
    (e) None of the above

47. Which one of the following is the result (in hexadecimal) of adding $2FFA_{16}$ and AB_{16}?
    (a) 30A5
    (b) 50A3
    (c) 2FFA5
    (d) 2FFAAB
    (e) None of the above

48. Which one of the following numbers is not the same as the other three?
    (a) 156_{10}
    (b) 1111_5
    (c) 10011100_2
    (d) 111_{16}
    (e) None of the above

49. Which one of the following binary fractions is equivalent to 0.1_{10}?
    - (a) 0.1_2
    - (b) 0.001_2
    - (c) 0.000111_2
    - (d) No finite binary representation possible

50. Which one of the following is equivalent to 0.110101_2?
    - (a) 0.65_8
    - (b) 0.66_8
    - (c) 0.56_8
    - (d) 0.814_{10}
    - (e) None of the above

51. Consider the floating-point 16-bit representation as described in Question 19 (that is sign + exponent + normalized mantissa). What does the floating-point representation 1010101010000111 represent?
    - (a) 0.1010101010000111
    - (b) 1010101.01
    - (c) 1010101010000111
    - (d) $-0.1010000111 \times 2^{-7}$
    - (e) None of the above

52. Which one of the following is equivalent to $ABCD_{16}$?
    - (a) 1100110111101111_2
    - (b) 13141516_8
    - (c) 23303132_4
    - (d) 43981_{10}
    - (e) None of the above

53. Which one of the following is correct?
    - (a) In ASCII encoding there is no distinction between upper and lower case characters.
    - (b) The MP3 audio format does not discard any information while compressing
    - (c) In Unicode a very large number of characters may be represented
    - (d) Using one byte for each of the RGB colours, a computer can represent up to 256 different colours
    - (e) None of the above is correct

54. Which of the following is the correct result of adding 2's complement numbers 11111110 and 00000010?
    - (a) 00000000
    - (b) 11111100
    - (c) 00000010
    - (d) 11111110
    - (e) None of the above

55. Which one of the following is the binary floating-point representation of 12.875_{10} if the floating-point format described above is used?
    - (a) 0110011100010100
    - (b) 0010100111000100
    - (c) 0001001000110100
    - (d) 1000100001100100

(e) None of the above

56. Which one of the following is the largest unsigned integer that can be represented using 16 bits?
   (a) 4,294,967,295
   (b) 65535
   (c) 1048575
   (d) 2,147,483,647
   (e) None of the above

57. Which one of the following is the largest signed integer that can be represented using 32 bits?
   (a) 4,294,967,295
   (b) 65535
   (c) 1048575
   (d) 2,147,483,647
   (e) None of the above

58. Which one of the following is NOT correct?
   (a) ZIP files do not lose any information in compression
   (b) A music CD usually has no compression on it
   (c) A video DVD usually has no compression on it
   (d) MP3 can reduce the size of a music file by a factor of 10
   (e) All of the above are correct

59. Which one of the following in NOT correct? Please do not convert numbers in one base to another; answer the question based only on visible inspection of the numbers.
   (a) 0.111111111_2 is equivalent to 0.777_8
   (b) 0.101101101_2 is equivalent to 0.555_8
   (c) 0.123_{16} is equivalent to 0.0001001001_2
   (d) 0.444_8 is equivalent to 0.011011011_2
   (e) All of the above are incorrect

5.3 Exercises

1. Consider the number 123. Find its value in base 5, 6 and 7.

2. Explain 2-complement and give an algorithm describing how it is used.

3. Explain the three different ways signed integers may be represented in a computer. Explain the differences between them and give reasons why one should be preferred over others.

4. Present the three components of a floating point system and discuss its advantages, Give some examples to show how it works.

5. What is EBSDIC and ASCII and what are their differences? Give one example of each code.

6. How many different numbers can be represented with a four digit number in a base six numbering system? Give the answer in decimal. Explain how you obtained your result.

7. Give the value of the largest 4 digit base six number in decimal and in base six representations.

8. Covert each of the following numbers to decimal values.

   a. 1011101_2

   b. 212101_3

   c. 13454_6

9. Draw an ordered table of all four-bit binary numbers and their equivalent values in decimal, octal and hexadecimal.

10. Write an addition table for a base 12 number system. Show only rows and columns with A and B.

11. Fill the addition table for a hexadecimal number system given below. The table only shows the rows and columns that involve A, B, C, D, E and F.

	A	B	C	D	E	F
A						
B						
C						
D						
E						
F						

12. Covert to binary: 526_8, 7014_8, $AC2_{16}$, $1D8E_{16}$ and 3021_4

13. How many bytes are there in a GigaBit, knowing that there are 8 bits in a byte and 1024 bytes in a KiloByte?

14. Finish the following binary arithmetic operations

   a.   11011001
       + 00111101

   b.   1011
       × 0101

15. Associate the following:

   i. 2^{10} bits

ii. 2^{30} bits

iii. 2^3 bits

iv. 2^{20} bits

v. 10^{-6} secs

vi. 10^{-12} secs

vii. 10^{-9} secs

viii. 10^{-3} secs

With these.

    a. gigabyte
    b. byte
    c. megabyte
    d. kilobyte
    e. nanosecond
    f. millisecond
    g. microsecond
    h. picosecond

16. A string of bits in a computer has no inherent meaning. Consider the bit pattern given below:

1100 0011 1001 0110

What does the above bit string represent if it was:

    a. an ASCII character string

    b. an unsigned integer

    c. a signed integer

    d. a two's complement integer

Explain your answers

17. Describe the ASCII and EBCDIC codes for representing symbols in a computer. How did they both originate? How many bits does each of them use? Which one is more widely used and why?

18. Describe the motivation for developing the Unicode encoding scheme. How many bits does it use and why? Describe the code. Is it being used currently? Give details.

19. Briefly describe the ISCII code. Is it being used widely? Is it best to use Unicode for the Indian languages? Why?

20. Estimate how many characters there are in this book. Now estimate how much memory it will take to store this book using ASCII, EBCDIC and Unicode.

21. Three customers walk into a café. The waiter comes to take their order. One of the customers does not want anything, one wants a hot chocolate, and the third wants a tea. How many different combinations of this order are possible? How many more would be possible if there were four customers and the fourth customer wanted a tea?

5.4 Answers to the Multiple Choice Questions

1. (a)
2. (b)
3. (b)
4. (a)
5. (d)
6. (a)
7. (a)
8. (c)
9. (b)
10. (e)
11. (a)
12. (b)
13. (b)
14. (c)
15. (b)
16. (b)
17. (d)
18. (a)
19. (a)
20. (e)
21. (b)
22. (a)
23. (b)
24. (c)
25. (e)
26. (d)
27. (d)
28. (d)
29. (d)
30. (d)
31. (a)
32. (b)
33. (a)
34. (a) and (c)
35. (a) and (c)
36. (d)
37. (e)
38. (e)
39. (b)
40. (d)
41. (b)
42. (d)
43. (c)
44. (a)
45. (d)
46. (c) and (d)
47. (a)

48. (d)
49. (d)
50. (a)
51. (d)
52. (d)
53. (c)
54. (a)
55. (a)
56. (b)
57. (d)
58. (c)
59. (d)

5.5 Brief Explanation of Multiple Choice Questions

1. All computer systems are based on the binary number system.

2. The place values of digits 1, 1, 1 and 1 from the left hand side are 8, 4, 2 and 1 respectively. Therefore (b) is correct.

3. The place values of each digit starting from the rightmost or least significant digit are b^0, b^1, b^2, and so on for base b. For base 6, the place values are 1, 6, 36, 216 and so on. Therefore (b) is correct.

4. The place values of digits in a fraction are b^{-1}, b^{-2}, b^{-3}, and so on for base b. Therefore, the place value of 3 is 4^{-3} or 1/6

5. The number $0111 = 0 + 4 + 2 + 1 = 7$

6. 255 is one less than 256 which is 100000000 and is therefore 1111 1111.

7. As explained in the last answer above 1111 1111 is 255.

8. 247 is 1111 0111 which is $128 + 64 + 32 + 16 + 0 + 4 + 2 + 1 = 127$. To convert to octal representation, we convert each set of three digests from the right into an octal digit. The first three digits on the right are 111 (7 octal), the next three are 110 (6 octal) leaving only 11 or 011 (3 octal). Therefore the representation is 367 and

9. The only place values that are the same are the least significant digits which all have a place value of 1.

10. To represent 1152_{10} into binary, we will need to use a bit corresponding to 2^{10} which is equal to 102 10 bits can represent numbers up to 1023 while the 11th bit has the place value 2^{10}. 10000000000 is therefore decimal 1024 which leaves 128 still to be represented. 128 is equal to 2^7 and therefore the binary representation for 1152 is 10010000000. For base 4, the place values are 1, 4, 16, 64, 256, 1024 and so on. To represent 1024 in base 4 we write 100000 and 128 is represented by 2000 so 1052 decimal is equivalent to 102000. Similarly, base 8 place values are 1, 8, 64, 512, 4096 and so on. In this case, 1024 is represented in base 8 as 2000 and 128 by 200 and therefore 1152 by 2200_8. Place values in base 12 are 1, 12, 144, 1728 and so on. 800_{12} therefore is $8 \times 144 = 1152_{10}$.

11. As noted earlier, $2^9 = 512_{10}$ and therefore the binary representation is the 10-bit long 1000000000.

12. The four digits in base 8 can be represented by 12 bits since each base 8 digit can be represented by 3 bits. In some cases the most significant bit or two bits can be zero which we can remove. In this case they are not since 7 is equivalent to 111.

13. 16 bits can represent the four digits in base 16 since 4 bits can represent each base 16 digit. In some cases the most significant bit or two bits can be zero which we can remove. In this case they are not since A is equivalent to 1010. Therefore 16 bits can be represented using 5 decimal digits.

14. As noted above, each hexadecimal digit can be represented by 4 bits and so 0001001000110100 can represent 123416. We can remove the leading zeros.

15. As noted earlier, each Octal digit can be represented by 3 bits and so 1234_8 can be represented by 001010011100. We can remove the leading zeros.

16. The result of adding 1110011 and 110011 is 10100110. Add starting from the least significant bits and carry 1 when adding 1 and 1.

17. The result of adding 10101010 and 110011 is 11011101. Add starting from the least significant bits and carry 1when adding 1 and 1.

18. Adding 777_8 and 666_8 is 1665_8. Starting from the least significant bits we first add 7 and 6 which gives 5_8 and a carry of 1. Then again adding 7 and 6 with a carry gives 6_8 with a carry of 1. The third addition gives16_8.

19. 1100.101010_2 is first normalised as 0.1100101010_2 times an exponent value of Since the number is positive, the sign bit is 0. Hence the floating point representation sign bit + exponent (5 bits) + normalized mantissa is 0 11001 1100101010. We have left spaces between the three components of the representation to help understanding. Therefore (a) is correct.

20. In this case, the given number 1100.10101010 has 12 bits although the last zero may be discarded. The remaining 11 bits cannot be represented in the given format without truncating the mantissa to 10 bits. If we decide to truncate then the problem becomes the same as the last one.

21. 128_{10} is equivalent to 10000000 or 0000000010000000 in 16 bits. Its one's complement is 1111111101111111, which represents -128_{10}.

22. In the last question, we found the one's complement of -128_{10}. 2's complement is obtained by adding 1 to it. Therefore, the 2's complement of 128_{10} in binary is 1111111110000000.

23. Only Unicode uses 16 bits to represent a character.

24. Audio information in computers and other devices is usually stored using MP3.

25. Floating-point representation includes a mantissa, an exponent, both normalized, to represent the number in a fixed number of bits.

26. A DVD can store compressed video which can store more than 100 minutes of video.

27. (c) is the correct answer since in adding two signed integer numbers the signs of the numbers must be taken into account.

28. To convert a binary number into hexadecimal, one needs to read the number from the right (not left) and replace each group of four bits by its equivalent hexadecimal digit. A byte is eight bits so it can store two hexadecimal digits. A number in any base can be converted to any other base. Floating-point representation can represent large integers but the size of the mantissa limits the number of digits that can be represented.

29. The only correct statement in this list is that there are two representations of zero using signed-magnitude numbers; +0 and -0.

30. There are no universally accepted standards for representing characters in a computer. There are also no universally accepted standards for representing Indian scripts. A code, Unicode, using 16 bits to represent a character has been developed. It provides codes for a very large number of character sets.

31. The original ASCII code was 7 bits. It was increased to 8 bits by including a parity bit.

32. The code of A in ASCII is hexadecimal 41, decimal 65 and binary 0100 0001. Therefore (b) is correct.

33. The code of 0 (zero) in ASCII is hexadecimal 30, decimal 48 and binary 0011 0000. Therefore (a) is correct.

34. 48_{10} is equivalent to 110000_2 and so is 60_8 but not 40_{16} since 40_{16} is equivalent to 64_{10}. 231_4 is equivalent to $2 \times 16 + 3 \times 4 + 1 = 45_{10}$. Therefore (a) and (c) are correct.

35. 31_{10} is equivalent to 11111_2, $1F_{16}$ but not 61_6 which is equivalent to decimal 37 and 31_8 is equivalent to 21_{10}. Therefore (a) and (c) are not equivalent to decimal 31.

36. One way to understand this question is as follows. $ABCDEF_{16}$ may be represented in 24 binary digits. 24 bits may be represented by 8 octal digits so (a) is correct. Similarly six bits may be represented by two octal digits so (b) is correct. Four base 32 digits may be represented in 20 bits which in turn may be represented by 5 hexadecimal digits, not eight. Therefore (c) is incorrect.

37. A RGB system in which each colour is represented by one byte is able to represent 256 x 256 x 256 different colours since one byte can represent 256 different numbers.

38. All are correct since audio signal has to be digitized for recording digitally. GIF uses only 256 colours while JPEG uses all the 16 million colour combinations. Since each pixel needs three bytes to store all the colours, a 3 Megapixel image needs 9 Mbytes to store.

39. The largest negative number using 16 bits is $- (2^{15} - 1)$ which is -32768. Therefore (b) is correct.

40. 1 is represented as 0000 0001. 1's complement of this number is 1111 1110 and 2's complement is 1111 1111. Therefore (d) is correct.

41. The place values of 3, 2, 0 and 1 are 1, 4, 16, and 64 respectively. The place values of 7, 6, 5 and 4 are 1, 6, 64 and 256. Therefore the two pairs in (b) are correct.

42. Since $2^{10} = 1024_{10}$ we have $2^{20} = 1024_{10} \times 1024_{10}$ which is slightly higher than a million. Therefore, 20 bits are needed to represent one million numbers and (d) is correct.

43. Since $2^{10} = 1024_{10}$ we have $2^{16} = 32_{10} \times 1024_{10}$ which is slightly higher than $32,000_{10}$. Therefore, 5 digits will be needed to represent the 16-bit binary number and (c) is correct.

44. The decimal number 123456 is a little bit smaller than 128,000 that is approximately equal to $2^{10} \times 2^8$. 18 bits will be needed to represent 123456_{10} and therefore (a) is correct.

45. 5 bits can represent each base 32 digit and so 0000100010001100100 can represent 1234_{32}. We can remove the leading zeros and therefore (d) is correct.

46. The representation of 791 in bases 2, 4, 8, and 16 is 1100010111, 30113, 1427 and 31 and therefore (c) and (d) are correct..

47. Adding 2FFA and AB using hexadecimal representation, we proceed as usual from right to left. A + B gives decimal 21 that using hexadecimal results in 5 and a carry of 1. Then F + A + 1 is decimal 26 which is A and a carry of 1. F + 1 decimal 16 which is 0 and a carry of 1. The last addition is now 2 + 1 = 3. Therefore the result is 30A5 and (a) is correct.

48. The first number is 156_{10}. The second 1111_5 is $125 + 25 + 5 + 1 = 156_{10}$ and the next 10011100_2 is $128 + 0 + 0 + 16 + 8 + 4 + 0 = 156_{10}$. The hexadecimal number 111_{16} is $256 + 16 + 1 = 273_{10}$. Therefore the odd number amongst the four is 111_{16} and (d) is the answer.

49. The place values of binary fraction are (in decimal) 0.5, 0.25, 0.125, 0.0625, 0.03125 (or ½, ¼, 1/16, 1/32, 1/64 etc) and so on. These will never add up to 0.1 (or 1/10). Try adding 6-7 values. Therefore the answer (d) is correct.

50. 0.110101_2 is equal to $½ + ¼ + 0 + 1/16 + 0 + 1/6$ The place values for digits in base 8 for a fraction are 1/8, 1/64 and so on. Since ½ is equal to 4 times 1/8, ¼ is equal to 2 times 1/8, and 1/16 is equal to 4 times 1/6 The last 1 is equivalent to 1/64 and therefore the equivalent octal representation is 0.65. Therefore the result is 0.65_8 and (a) is correct.

51. First break the floating –point number in the three components. Starting from the left 1 (sign bit, negative), 01010 (exponent is 9, subtract 16 and get -7), mantissa is 1010000111. The number therefore in binary is $-0.1010000111 \times 2^{-7}$. Therefore (d) is correct.

52. (a) is equivalent to $CDEF_{16}$ since 1100 is 12. (b) $1314151 6_8$ is equal to $BCDE_{16}$ since octal 13 is hex B. (c) 23303132_4 is also $BCDE_{16}$ since 23_4 is B_{16}. (d) is equivalent to $ABCD_{16}$ since it in decimal representation is equivalent to $10 \times 16 \times 16 \times 16 + 11 \times 16 \times 16 + 12 \times 16 + 13$ which is 43981. Therefore (d) is correct.

53. Unicode uses 16 bits for each character and can therefore represent a large number of characters; Eight bits can represent only 256 different characters while 16 bits can represent 256 x 256 characters.

54. If we add 11111110 and 0000000010, the addition starts from the right as usual. The first bit after addition is $0 + 0 = 0$ and the second bit is $1 + 1 = 0$ carry 1. This carry 1 results in all remaining additions becoming 0 with a carry 1 which eventually is discarded at the final addition of the most significant bits. Therefore the correct answer is (a).

55. Let us first convert 12.875_{10} to binary. Decimal 12 is equal to 1100_2 and 0.875_{10} is equal to 0.111_2 (since $0.875 = 0.5 + 0.25 + 0.125$). Therefore 12.875 is equal to 1100.111_2. Normalized mantissa is 0.1100111 and the exponent is 4 which will be represented by 16 + The floating-point representation therefore is 0110011100010100.

56. 16 bits can represent unsigned numbers up to 2^{16}-1, which is 65535. Therefore the correct answer is (b).

57. 32 bits with a sign can represent numbers up to 2^{31}-1, which is +2,147,483,647. Therefore (d) is correct.

58. A video DVD does use compression so (c) is the answer.

59. We need to know the place values of digits after the radix point. For binary, the place values are ½, ¼, 1/8, and so on. For octal the values are 1/8, 1/64, 1/256 and so on. For hexadecimal, the values are 1/16, 1/256, and so on. Therefore 0.111111111_2 is equivalent to 0.777_8. 0.101101101_2 is equivalent 0.555_8. 123_{16} is equivalent to 0.000100100011_2. 0.444_8 is equivalent to 0.100100100_2 and not 0.011011011_2. Therefore (d) is incorrect and is the answer.

5.6 Solutions to the First Five Exercises

1. Consider the number 123. Find its value in base 5, 6 and 7.

- Base 5

  $4 + 3 \times 5 + 2 \times 5 \times 5 + 5 \times 5 \times 5 = 4 + 15 + 50 + 125 = 194$

- Base 6

  $4 + 3 \times 6 + 2 \times 6 \times 6 + 6 \times 6 \times 6 = 4 + 18 + 72 + 216 = 210$

- Base 7

  $4 + 3 \times 7 + 2 \times 7 \times 7 + 7 \times 7 \times 7 = 4 + 21 + 98 + 343 = 466$

2. Explain 2-complement and give an algorithm describing how it is used.

   Two's complement for a binary number can be obtained by flipping the bits of a given binary number and adding 1 to it. Thus 0011's two's complement is 1101 (1100 + 1) and that of 11100110 is 00011010 (00011001 + 1). The beauty of complement number schemes is that computer arithmetic does not need to worry about the sign of the number. To add two numbers, we just add the 2's complement representation of the numbers and discard any carry.

3. Explain the three different ways signed integers may be represented in a computer. Explain the differences between them and give reasons why one should be preferred over others.

   Signed integer - Since a sign – or + cannot be represented within a computer, one convenient way to represent sign is to use the leftmost or the most significant bit in the storage area (the storage area may be 16, 32 or 64 bits) to indicate the number's sign. Often a 1 in this bit is used to indicate a negative number.

   1's complement - Any binary number has a 1's complement number that has the 1's in the original binary number replaced by 0's and 0's replaced by 1's. For example, 5 in binary is 0101 and its complement is 1010 which is –5 in that column. This is 1's complement.

   2's complement - Two's complement for a binary number can be obtained by flipping the bits of a given binary number and adding 1 to it. Thus 0011's two's complement is 1101 (1100 + 1) and that of 11100110 is 00011010 (00011001 + 1).

   The beauty of complement number schemes is that computer arithmetic does not need to worry about the sign of the number. To add two numbers, we just add the 2's complement representation of the numbers and discard any carry. For 1's complement, we add the two numbers and add the carry to the remaining number.

4. Present the three components of a floating point system and discuss its advantages, Give some examples to show how it works.

   The floating-point representation of real numbers is composed of the sign, the mantissa value and the exponent value. The numbers are usually normalised by adjusting the exponent to ensure that the mantissa value is between 1 and the number base being used (2 in binary representation). The normalisation allows best use of a given number of mantissa digits, allowing very large and very small numbers to be represented to about the same percentage precision. In binary representation, the mantissa occupies the major part of the fixed length floating point number with the exponent occupying the remaining bits.

5. What is EBSDIC and ASCII and what are their differences? Give one example of each code.

EBCDIC (Extended Binary Coded Decimal Interchange Code) developed by IBM and ASCII (American Standard Code for Information Interchange) set as a standard by the US government. ASCII is a 7-bit code while EBCDIC is an 8-bit code used on large IBM mainframes. EBCDIC code was developed in the mid-1960s. ASCII is a 7-bit code and information in a computer is normally grouped in 8-bit bytes, ISO decided to use the eighth bit for error detection. The approach used is called parity checking. Parity checking is a simple and basic error checking technique by which the parity bit (the eighth bit) is either turned on or off depending on whether the sum of the other seven bits is even or odd.